HOW TO START
DAY TRADE
FOR BEGINNERS

Day Trading Strategies to become a Profitable Investor and Build a Passive Income! Amazing Secrets Of How to Day Trade for a Living

- VOL.2 -

DEVERA JONES

Table of Contents

Strategy 1: ABCD Pattern

The ABCD Pattern is one of the most basic and easiest patterns to trade, and it is an excellent choice for beginner and intermediate traders. Although it is simple and has been known for a long time, it still works effectively because so many traders are still trading it. As mentioned earlier, it has a self-fulfilling prophecy effect. You should do whatever all of the other traders are doing because a trend is your friend. A trend may very well be your only friend in the market.

Let's take a look at this pattern in Figure 7.1:

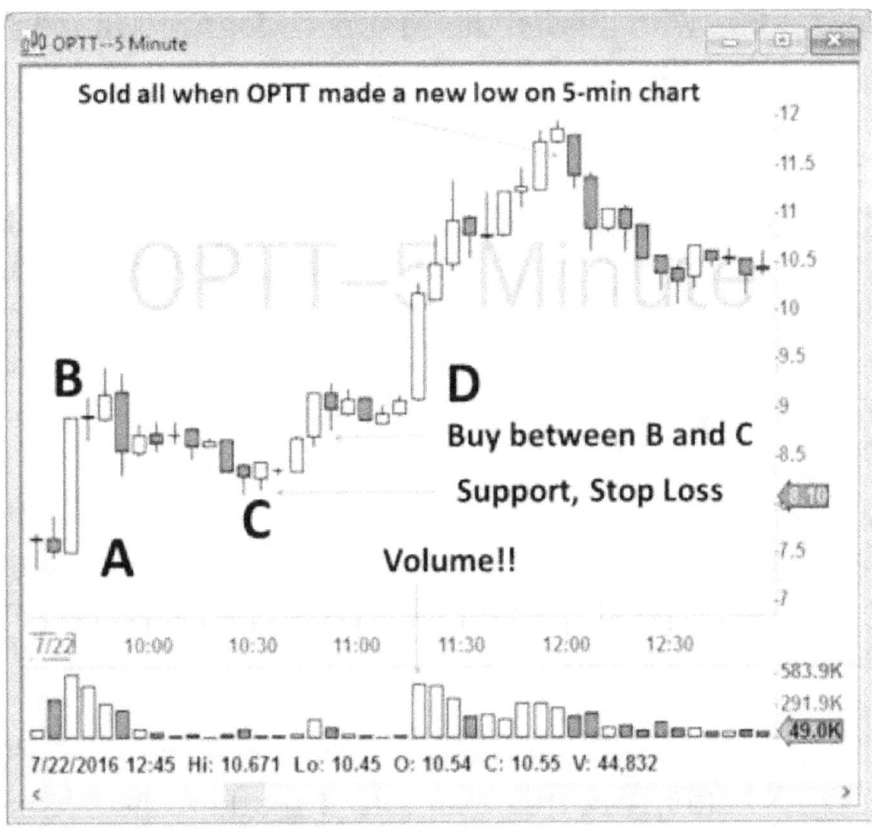

Figure 7.1 - Example of an ABCD Pattern.

ABCD Patterns start with a strong upward move. Buyers are aggressively buying a stock from point A and making constantly new highs of the day (point B). You want to enter the trade, but you should not chase the trade, because at point B it is very extended and already at a high price. In addition, you cannot say where your stop loss should be. You must never enter a trade without knowing where your stop is.

At point B, traders who bought the stock earlier start slowly selling it for profit and the price comes down. You should still not enter the trade because you do not know where the bottom of this pull back will be. However, if you see that the price does not come down from a certain level, such as point C, it means that the stock has found a potential support. Therefore, you can plan your trade and set up stops and a profit taking point.

The above screenshot, marked as Figure 7.1, is of Ocean Power Technologies Inc. (ticker: OPTT) at July 22, 2016, when they announced that they had a new $50 million contract to build a new ship (There's a fundamental catalyst! Remember Chapter 2?).

The stock surged up from $7.70 (A) to $9.40 (B) at around 9:40 a.m. I, along with many other traders who missed the first push higher, waited for point B and then a confirmation that the stock wasn't going to go lower than a certain price (point C). When I saw that point C was holding as a support and that buyers would not let the stock price go any lower than $8.10 (C), I bought 1,000 shares of OPTT near C, with my stop being a break below point C. I knew that when the price went higher, closer to B, buyers would jump on massively. As I mentioned before, the ABCD Pattern is a very classic strategy and many retail traders look for it. Close to point D, the volume suddenly spiked, which meant that many more traders were jumping into the trade.

My profit target was when the stock made a new low on a 5-minute chart, which was a sign of weakness. As you can see in Figure 7.1, OPTT had a nice run up to around $12 and showed weakness by making a new low on a 5-minute chart at around $11.60. That is when I sold all of my position.

Figure 7.2 is another example, this time for SPU on August 29, 2016. There are actually two ABCD Patterns in this example. I marked the second one as *abcd pattern*. Usually, as the trading day progresses, volumes become lower and therefore the second pattern is smaller in size. Please note that you will always have high volumes at points B and D (and in this instance also at points b and d).

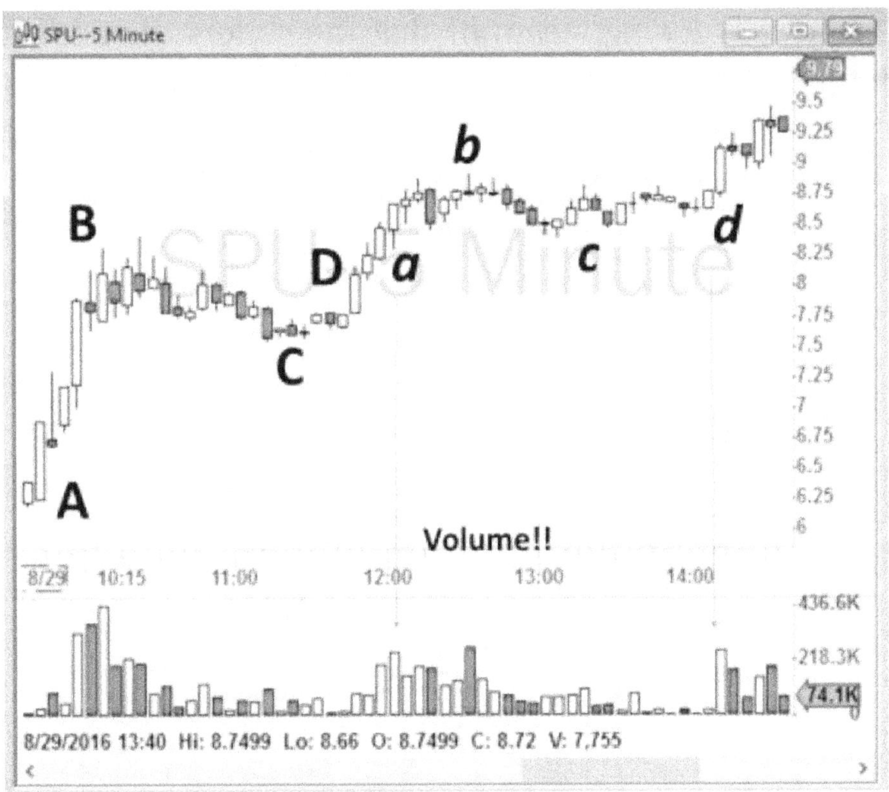

Figure 7.2 - Example of ABCD Pattern and abcd pattern.

To summarize my trading strategy for the ABCD Pattern:

1. When I observe with my scanner or I'm advised by someone in our chatroom that a stock is surging up from point A and reaching a significant new high for the day (point B), I wait to see if the price makes a support higher than point A. I call this point C. I do not jump into the trade right away.
2. I watch the stock during its consolidation period (I'll explain this term in the next strategy). I choose my share size and stop and exit strategy.
3. When I see that the price is holding support at level C, I enter the trade close to the price of point C in anticipation of moving forward to point D or higher.
4. My stop is the loss of point C. If the price goes lower than point C, I sell and accept the loss. Therefore, it is important to buy the stock close to point C to minimize the loss. Some traders wait and buy only at point D to ensure that the ABCD Pattern is really working. In my opinion, that approach basically reduces your reward while at the same time increasing your risk.
5. If the price moves higher, I sell half of my position at point D, and bring my stop higher to my entry point (break-even).
6. I sell the remaining position as soon as my target hits or I sense that

the price is losing steam or that the sellers are acquiring control of the price action. When the price makes a new low on my 5-minute chart, it is a good indicator that the buyers are almost exhausted.

Strategy 2: Bull Flag Momentum

In day trading, Bull Flag is a Momentum Strategy that usually works very effectively on low float stocks under $10 (Chapter 4). This trading strategy is difficult to manage the risk in and requires a fast execution platform.

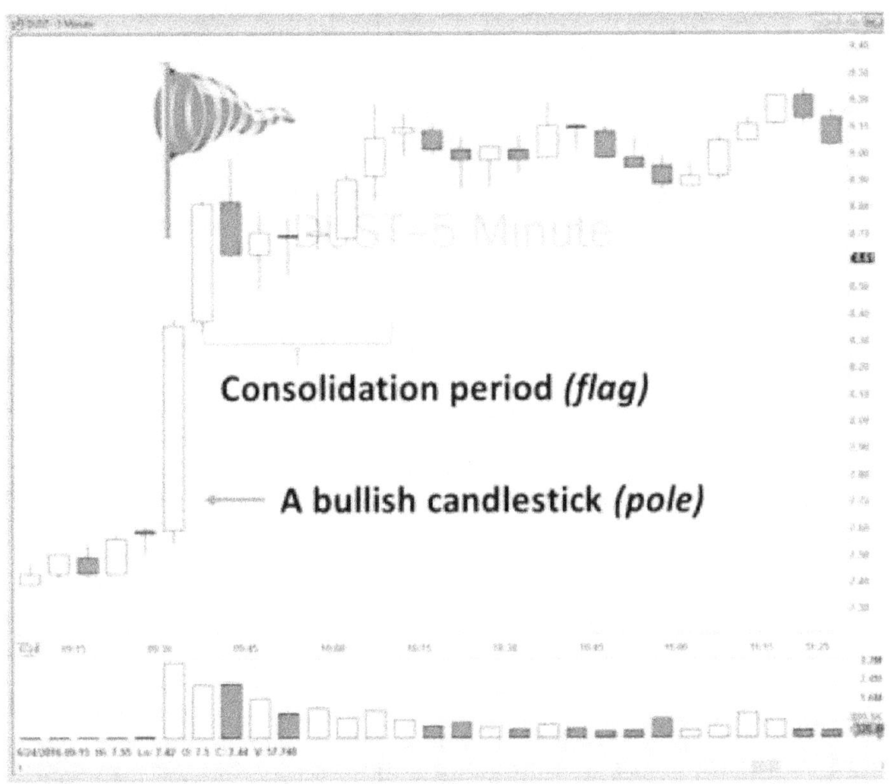

Figure 7.3 - Example of Bull Flag formation with one consolidation period.

This pattern, shown above in Figure 7.3, is named Bull Flag because it resembles a flag on a pole. In Bull Flag, you have several large candles going up (like a pole), and you also have a series of small candles moving sideways (like a flag), or, as we day traders say, "consolidating". Consolidation means that the traders who bought stocks at a lower price are now selling and taking their profits. Although that is happening, the price does not decrease sharply because the buyers are still entering into trades and the sellers are not yet in control of the price. Many traders who missed buying the stock before the Bull Flag started, will now be looking for an opportunity to take a trade. Wise traders know that it is risky to buy a stock when the price is increasing significantly. That's called *"chasing the stock"*. Professional traders aim to enter the trade during quiet times and take their profits during the wild times. That, of course, is the total opposite of how amateurs trade. They jump in or out when stocks begin to run, but grow bored and lose interest when the prices are, shall I say, sleepy.

Chasing the stocks is an account killer for beginners. You must wait until the stock finds its high point, and then you must wait for the consolidation. As soon as the price start breaking up in the consolidation area, you can begin purchasing stocks. Patience truly is a virtue.

Usually a Bull Flag will show several consolidation periods. I enter in only during the first and second consolidation periods. Third and higher consolidation periods are risky because the price has probably been very extended in a way that indicates that the buyers will soon be losing their control. Let's study an example in Figure 7.4 below of a Bull Flag on RIGL on August 30, 2016.

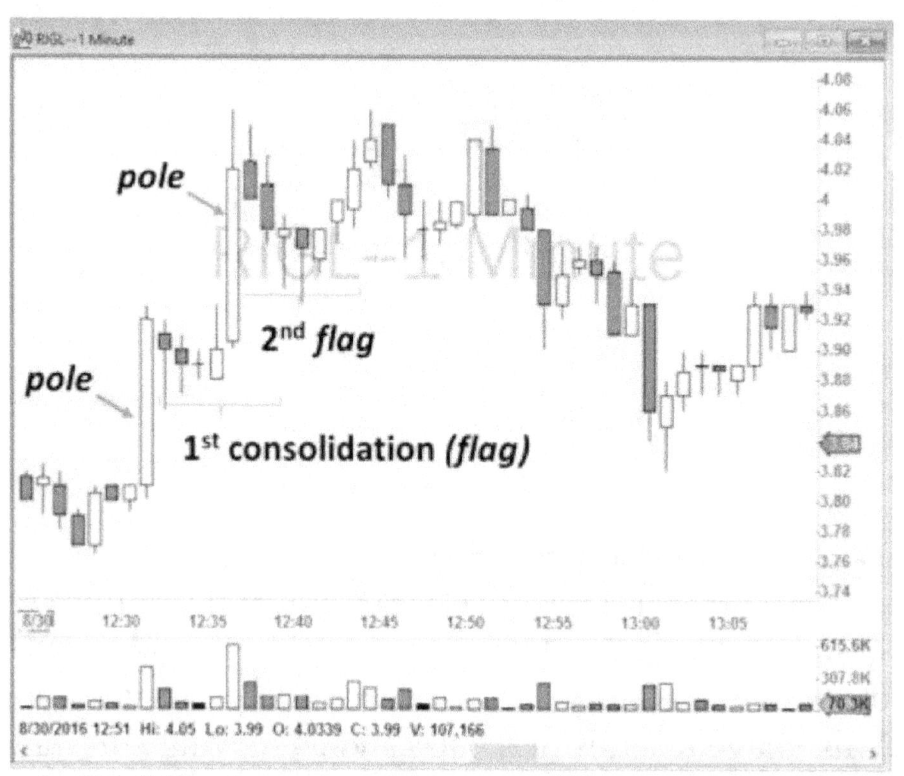

Figure 7.4 - Example of Bull Flag formation with two consolidation periods on RIGL.

This is an example of two Bull Flag Patterns. It is normally hard to catch the first Bull Flag, and you will probably miss it, but your scanner should alert you to it so that you can be ready for the next Bull Flag. Figure 7.5 that follows is an example from my scanner in this time period:

History: Intraday Bull Flag Momentum Scalping Strategy

Time	Symbol	Price ($)	Vol Today	Rel Vol	Flt (3hr)	Vol 5 Min	Strategy Name
12:45:00 PM	CELP	8.68	53,491	2.70	4.26M	4,059	Strong Low-Float Bull Flag Momentum
12:38:51 PM	RESN	5.66	88,841		5.63M	2,168	Strong Low-Float Bull Flag Momentum
12:36:15 PM	RIGL	3.94	42.49M	120.83	89.1M	4,111	Medium-Float Bull Flag Momentum
12:34:53 PM	ITEK	7.16	659,979	7.18	13.2M	19.3K	Medium-Float Bull Flag Momentum
12:31:52 PM	RIGL	3.91	41.87M	120.97	89.1M	3,394	Medium-Float Bull Flag Momentum
12:29:30 PM	KPTI	9.42	1.47M	22.72	3.93M	1,456	Low-Float Bull Flag Momentum
12:29:30 PM	KPTI	9.39	1.47M	22.72	3.93M	1,445	Low-Float Bull Flag Momentum
12:12:37 PM	AMID	12.08	2.62M	28.09		55.5K	+$10 Strong Bull Flag Momentum
11:57:44 AM	LNTH	9.96	604,695	4.84	11.3M	543.7	Medium-Float Bull Flag Momentum
11:56:42 AM	LNTH	9.95	599,426	4.83	11.3M	569.0	Medium-Float Bull Flag Momentum
11:51:04 AM	BIOL	1.81	224,633	6.43	32.4M	2,353	Medium-Float Bull Flag Momentum

Figure 7.5 - Example of my intraday Bull Flag Strategy.

As you can see, my scanner showed RIGL at 12:36:15 p.m. As soon as I saw that, I realized that there was also a very high relative volume of trading (120 times the normal trading volume), which made this a perfect setup for day trading. I waited for the first consolidation period to finish and, as soon as the stock started to move toward its high for the day, I jumped into the trade. My stop loss was the breakdown of the consolidation period. I marked my exit and entry on Figure 7.6 below.

Figure 7.6 - Entry, stop and exit of a Bull Flag Strategy on RIGL.

You can see the Bull Flag Pattern on any short time frame: 1-minute, 2-minute and 5-minute charts. Now let's take a look at Figure 7.7, a 2-minute chart for

OPTT on June 1, 2016. As you can see, the stock had a powerful Bull Flag right at the Open, followed by a consolidation period. As soon as the first consolidation period was completed, another small Bull Flag formed. The volume of shares traded is significantly higher after consolidation, which is a confirmation for a long entry.

You can also see another Bull Flag in the OPTT 2-minute chart followed by another consolidation period. As shown below in Figure 7.7, after the second consolidation period, the volume of shares traded was significantly higher, a confirmation for another long entry. I don't trade more than two Bull Flags in a stock and, as you can see in this chart, the stock started to sell off after the third Bull Flag (at around $7). Aside from the strategy, did you notice that OPTT moved from $1.50 to almost $7 in just 35 minutes? This kind of move can be expected from low float under $10 stocks.

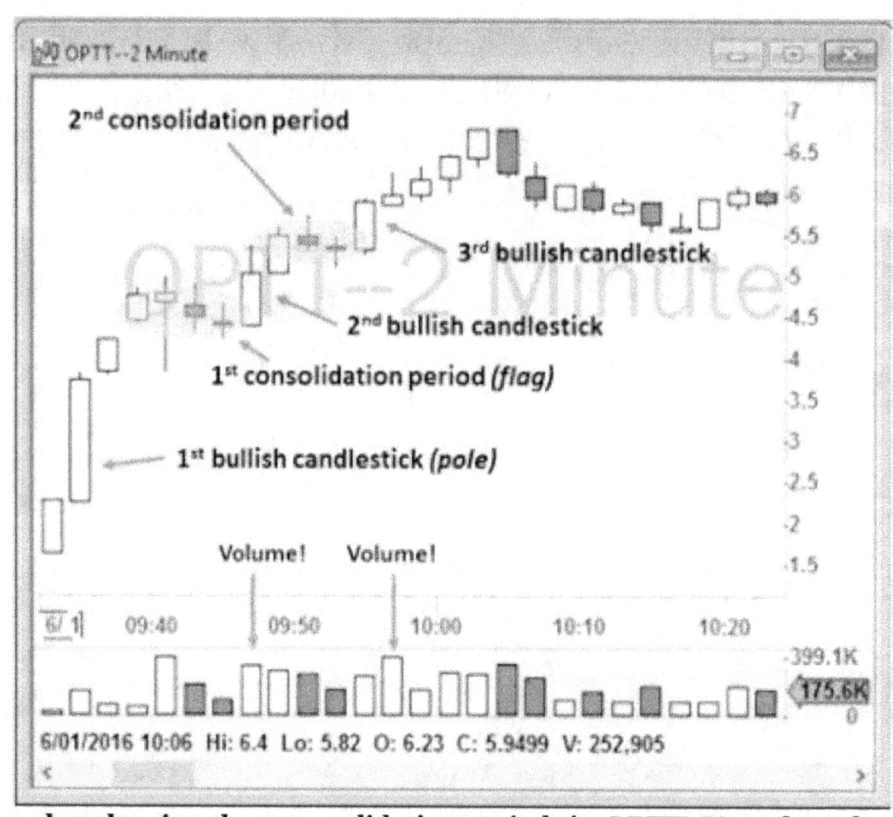

Figure 7.7 - Screenshot showing three consolidation periods in OPTT. Note the volume increases after each consolidation period.

To summarize my trading strategy:

1. When I see a stock surging up (either on my scanner or when advised by someone in our chatroom), I patiently wait until the consolidation period. I do not jump into the trade right away (you

will recall that is the dangerous act of "chasing the stock").
2. I watch the stock during the consolidation period. I choose my share size and stop and exit strategy.
3. As soon as prices are moving over the high of the consolidation candlesticks, I enter the trade. My stop loss is the break below the consolidation periods.
4. I sell half of my position and take a profit on the way up. I bring my stop loss from the low of the consolidation to my entry price (break-even).
5. I sell my remaining positions as soon as my target hits or I sense that the price is losing steam and the sellers are gaining control of the price action.

The Bull Flag is essentially an ABCD Pattern that will happen more often on low float stocks. However, in a Bull Flag Strategy for stocks under $10, many traders buy only at or near the breakout (opposite to the ABCD Pattern for medium float stocks). The reason for this is because moves in low float stocks are fast and they will fade away very quickly. Therefore, Bull Flag is more or less a *Momentum and Scalping Strategy*. Scalpers buy when a stock is running. They rarely like to buy during consolidation (during that waiting and holding phase). These types of stocks usually drop quickly and brutally so it is important to jump in only when there is a confirmation of breakout. Waiting for the stock to break the top of a consolidation area is a way of reducing your risk and exposure time in low float stocks. Instead of buying and holding and waiting, which increases exposure time, scalpers just wait for the breakout and then send their order. Get in, scalp, and get out quickly. That's the philosophy of momentum scalpers:

- Get in at the breakout
- Take your profit
- Get out of the way

The Bull Flag Pattern is found within an uptrend in a stock. The Bull Flag is a long-based strategy. You should not short a Bull Flag. I personally don't trade much momentum. It is a risky strategy and beginners should be very careful trading these. If you choose to, trade only in a small size and only after sufficient practice in simulators. You will also need a super-fast execution system for scalping.

Strategies 3 and 4: Reversal Trading

Top and Bottom Reversals are two other trading strategies that day traders love using because they have very defined entry and exit points. In this section, I'm going to explain how to find reversal setups using scanners, how to use indecision or Doji candlesticks to take an entry, how to understand where to set your stops and your profit targets, and how to trail your winners.

If you are part of our chatroom, you will hear me say time and time again that what goes up, must come down. *Don't chase the trade if it is too extended.* The inverse is also true. What goes down will definitely come back up to some extent. When a stock starts to sell off significantly, there are two reasons behind it:

1. Institutional traders and hedge funds have started selling their large position to the public market and the stock price is tanking.
2. Traders have started short selling a stock because of some bad fundamental news, but they will have to cover their shorts sooner or later. That is where you wait for an entry. When short sellers are trying to cover their shorts, the stock will reverse quickly, that is called a "short squeeze". You want to ride that.

I'm going to illustrate this strategy with a few examples so that you can see exactly what to look for. Figure 7.8 below is an example of what it looks like to find a stock that has sold off really hard right after the market opens. Moves like this are extremely hard to catch for the short side, because when you find the stock, it is already too late to enter the short selling trade. But please, remember the mantra: *what goes up, must come down.* Therefore, you have the option of waiting for a reversal opportunity.

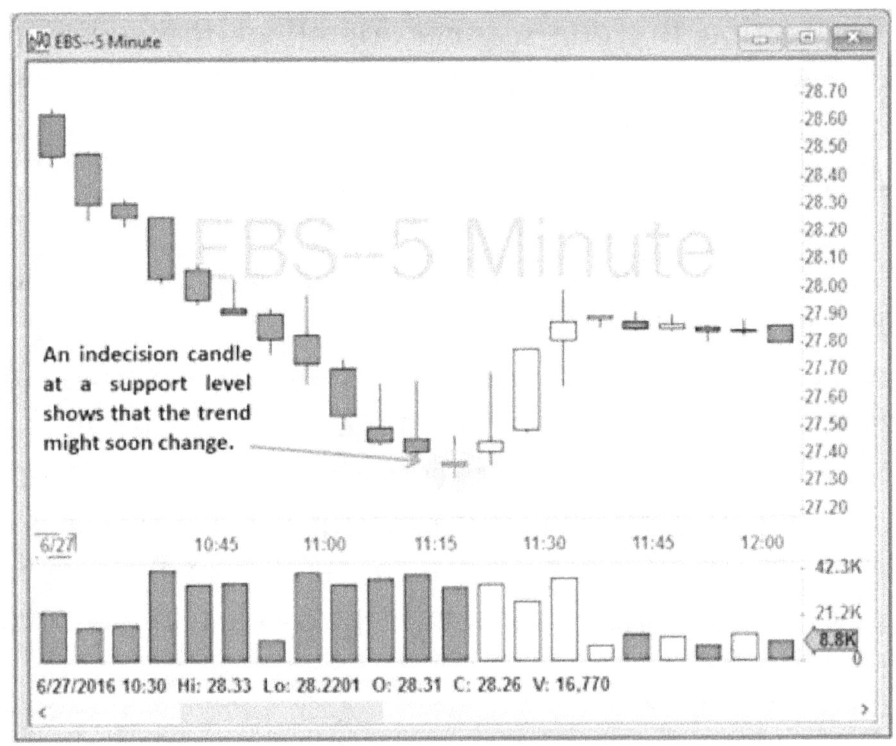

Figure 7.8 - Example of a Reversal Strategy on EBS.

Each Reversal Strategy has four important elements:

1. At least five candlesticks on a 5-minute chart moving upward or downward.
2. The stock will have an extreme 5-minute RSI indicator (Relative Strength Index). An RSI above 90 or below 10 will pique my interest. The RSI, developed initially by famous technical analyst Welles Wilder, Jr., is an indicator that compares the magnitude of recent gains and losses in price over a period of time to measure the speed and change of price movement. The RSI values range from 0 to 100. Traders in Reversal Strategies use RSI values to identify overbought or oversold conditions and to find buy or sell signals. For example, RSI readings above 90 indicate overbought conditions and RSI readings below 10 indicate oversold conditions. If you want to learn more about the RSI indicator, you can do a Google search or ask me in the chatroom. Your trading platform or scanner software calculates RSI automatically for you.

These two elements demonstrate that a stock is really stretched out, and you must pay close attention to your scanner for all of these data points. I have configured my scanner to highlight RSIs lower than 20 and higher than 80 so I can very quickly recognize them. You must simultaneously look for a certain RSI level and a certain number of consecutive candles.

3. The stock is being traded at or near an important intraday support or resistance level. For details of how to find support or resistance levels, please read my commentary that follows for support or resistance trading. I only take reversal trades when the price is near a significant support level (for Bottom Reversal) or a significant resistance level (for Top Reversal).
4. When the trend is coming to an end, usually indecision candles, such as a spinning top or Doji, form. That is when you need to be ready.

In reversal trading, you are looking for one of the indecision candlesticks that we reviewed in Chapter 6. They are an indication that the trend may soon change. A Doji is a candle that has a wick longer than its body. You can see a picture of a bearish Doji in Figure 7.9 below. It has that long upper wick that some would call a top tail and that others would call a shooting star. This candle tells you four things: the open price, the close price, the high of that period and the low of that period. So, when you have a candle with a top tail, you know that at some point during that candle period the price moved up, was unable to hold at that level, and was then sold off. It depicts a bit of a battle taking place between the buyers and the sellers in which the buyers lost their push up. It is a good indication that the sellers may soon control the price and will push that price down.

The same is true about a bullish Doji. You can also see a picture of a bullish Doji in Figure 7.9 below. It has that long lower wick that some would call a bottom tail and others would call a hammer. When you have a hammer candle with a bottom tail, you know that at some point during that candle period the price moved down, was unable to hold at those low levels, and was bought up. This indicates a battle between the buyers and the sellers in which the sellers lost their push down. It is a good indication that the buyers may now gain control of the price and push that price up.

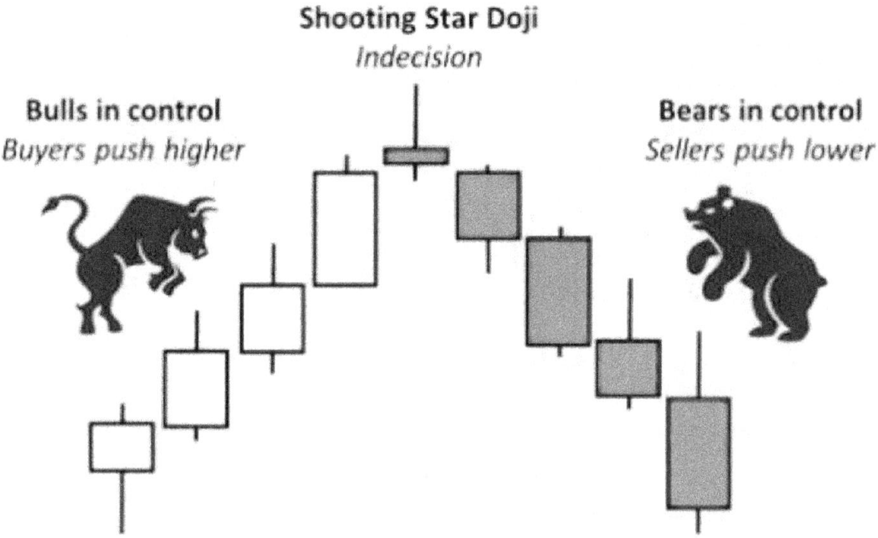

Figure 7.9 - Top Reversal Strategy with an indecision Shooting star candlestick formed as a sign of entry.

In reversal trading, you look for either Doji or indecision candlesticks. They are an indication that the trend may soon change. In Reversal Strategies, you are looking for a clear confirmation that the pattern is beginning to reverse. What you definitely don't want is to be on the wrong side of a reversal trade, or, as we call it, "*catching a falling knife*". It doesn't sound like a good idea in real life and it's not a good idea in trading. It means that when a stock is selling off badly (the falling knife), you don't want to buy on the assumption that it should bounce. If the stocks are dropping, you want to wait for the confirmation of the reversal. This will usually be (1) the formation of a Doji or indecision candle and (2) the first 1-minute or the first 5-minute candle to reach a new high near an important intraday support level. That is my entry point. I set my stop at the low of the previous candlestick or at the loss of the support level.

In reversal trading, it is best that the RSI be at the extremes (above 90, below 10). Once you find that, you must then look for an actual entry near a strong intraday support (for Bottom Reversal) or resistance level (for Top Reversal). As mentioned, an entry for me is going to be either the first 1-minute or the first 5-minute candle to reach a new high (for Bottom Reversal) or to make a new low (for Top Reversal) and only when the price is being traded near an important intraday support or resistance level.

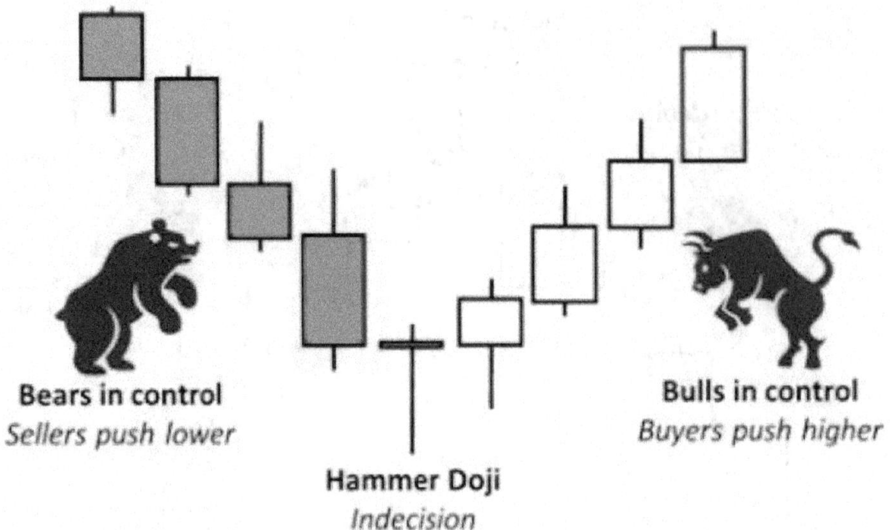

Figure 7.10 - Bottom Reversal Strategy with an indecision hammer candlestick formed as a sign of entry.

In a Bottom Reversal, when you've had a long run of consecutive candles making new lows, the first candle that makes the new high near an important support level is very significant. That's my entry point. There are times when I'll use the 1-minute chart, but typically I'll wait for the 5-minute chart because it is a much better confirmation. The 5-minute chart is cleaner. The first 5-minute candle to make a new high near an intraday support level is the point at which I enter the reversal, with a stop at the low of the day.

Once you're in one of these trades, your exit indicators are quite simple. I take profit when the price reaches a moving average (either 9 EMA, 20 EMA or VWAP) or reaches another important intraday level.

In a Bottom Reversal, if the stock pops up and then suddenly moves back down, I stop out for a loss. If I jump in long, buying stock and hoping the price will go higher, and instead the price ends up just going sideways, it's a sign that I am probably going to see a consolidation for another move down, and that is an indication that the price is probably going to continue to drop. If I get in and I hold for a few minutes and the price stays flat, I get out, no matter what happens after that. I may be wrong, but I don't like to expose my account to the unknown. I need to be in the right setup, and if it is not ready yet, I'm out. If I get into the profit zone, I can start adjusting my stop, first to break-even, and then to the low of the last 5-minute candle. I will then keep adjusting my stop as I move up.

In Reversal Strategies, one of the main tasks of a trader is to watch stocks that are running up or down, while simultaneously identifying possible support or resistance levels and areas that could provide a good reversal opportunity on daily charts. This allows you to resist being impulsive and rushing into the trade. Instead, you wait for the areas of stagnation. You take your time and watch the trade develop and wait for the reversal to begin.

Bottom Reversal

This beautiful illustration that follows in Figure 7.11 is on Emergent BioSolutions Inc. (ticker: EBS) and shows a perfect reversal that I found using my stock scanners. An indecision candlestick at the bottom of the downtrend signifies a potential reversal, and, as you can see, right after that is a big swing back up. I took this trade right after seeing an indecision Doji, and kept my stop at the low of that indecision candlestick. When EBS hit my scanner, I quickly changed my chart to a daily one and found important nearby support and resistance levels of $27.36 and $28. As mentioned previously, to learn how to find support and resistance levels, please read further along in this chapter.

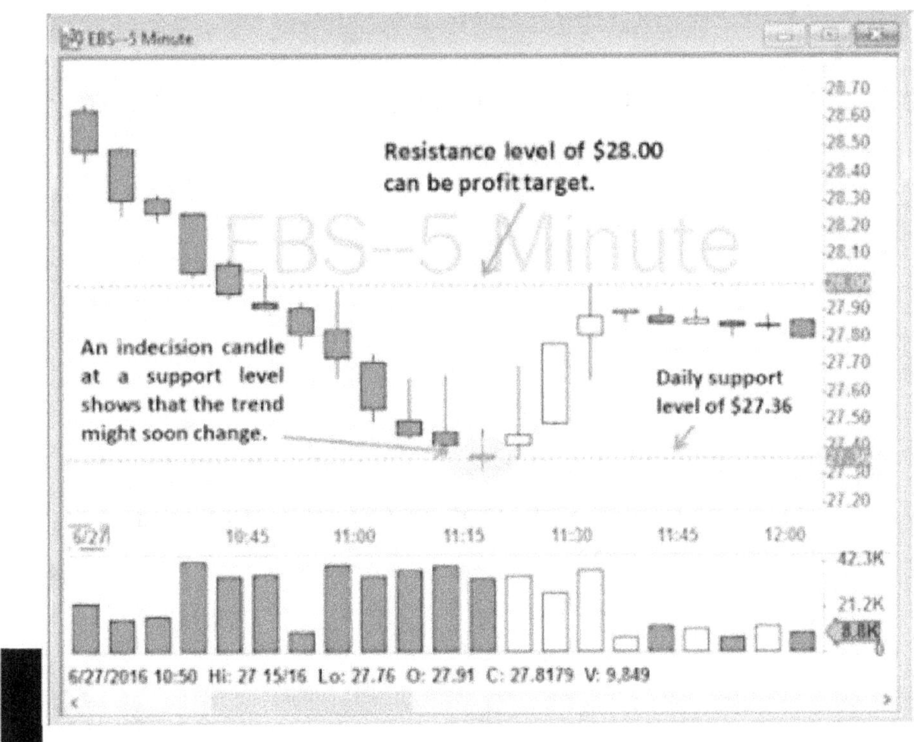

Figure 7.11 - Example of a Reversal Strategy on EBS.

The most significant advantage to Reversal Strategies is that they overcome the difficulty of anticipating when stocks will make major moves. You will probably miss the moment when the stock starts to sell off, and you won't have time to sell short the stock for profit, but you can always prepare for the reversal trade.

Another example of a Bottom Reversal Strategy is in Figure 7.12 that follows:

Figure 7.12 - Example of a Bottom Reversal Strategy on ALR.

I found Alere Inc. (ticker: ALR) on June 27, 2016 at 10:57 a.m. using my Trade Ideas real time Bottom Reversal scanner. See the image below in Figure 7.13:

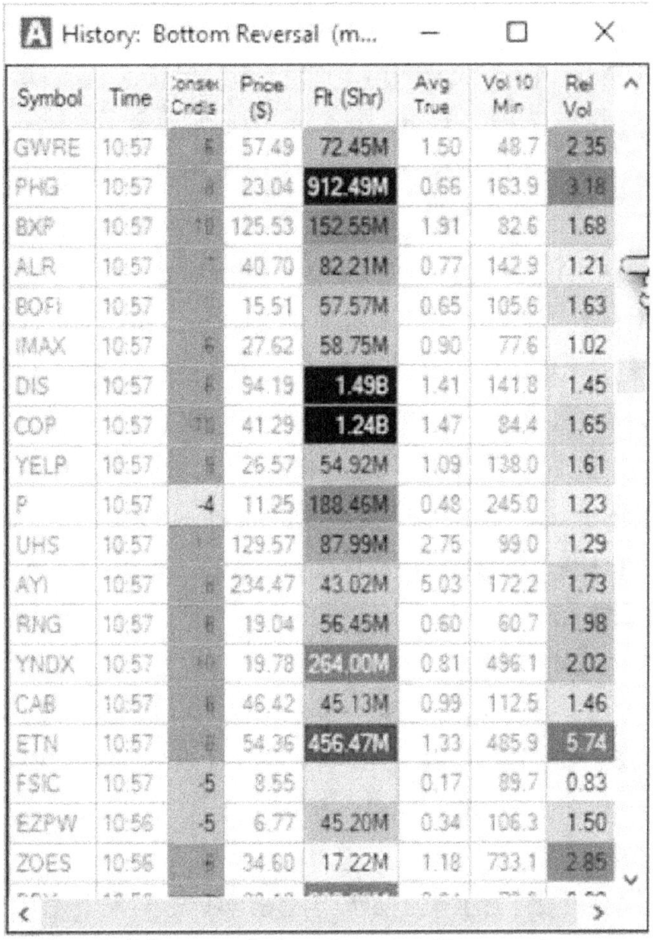

Symbol	Time	Consec Cndls	Price ($)	Flt (Shr)	Avg True	Vol 10 Min	Rel Vol
GWRE	10:57		57.49	72.45M	1.50	48.7	2.35
PHG	10:57		23.04	912.49M	0.66	163.9	3.18
BXP	10:57		125.53	152.55M	1.91	82.6	1.68
ALR	10:57		40.70	82.21M	0.77	142.9	1.21
BOFI	10:57		15.51	57.57M	0.65	105.6	1.63
IMAX	10:57		27.62	58.75M	0.90	77.6	1.02
DIS	10:57		94.19	1.49B	1.41	141.8	1.45
COP	10:57		41.29	1.24B	1.47	84.4	1.65
YELP	10:57		26.57	54.92M	1.09	138.0	1.61
P	10:57	-4	11.25	188.46M	0.48	245.0	1.23
UHS	10:57		129.57	87.99M	2.75	99.0	1.29
AYI	10:57		234.47	43.02M	5.03	172.2	1.73
RNG	10:57		19.04	56.45M	0.60	60.7	1.98
YNDX	10:57		19.78	264.00M	0.81	496.1	2.02
CAB	10:57		46.42	45.13M	0.99	112.5	1.46
ETN	10:57		54.36	456.47M	1.33	485.9	5.74
FSIC	10:57	-5	8.55		0.17	89.7	0.83
EZPW	10:56	-5	6.77	45.20M	0.34	106.3	1.50
ZOES	10:56		34.60	17.22M	1.18	733.1	2.85

Figure 7.13 - Example of my Trade Ideas real time Bottom Reversal scanner showing ALR with seven consecutive downward candlesticks.

My scanner, at 10:57 a.m., showed me that ALR had seven consecutive candles to the downside, a relatively low float (80 million shares) and a relative volume of 1.21, which meant it was trading higher than usual. I actually did not take this trade because I missed my entry, but I wanted to show you what overall trading strategies look like for Bottom Reversals. If you look again at the above Figure 7.12, the screenshot of ALR's daily chart, you will see a significant intraday level of support at $40.67. The price reversed at that level with higher than usual trading volume. Please note that no indecision candlestick formed in this reversal. Instead, the reversal was indicated by a strong bullish candlestick (marked on the above Figure 7.12). At times, a reversal happens so fast that indecision candlesticks will not form. Therefore, it is important to observe the price action near significant intraday levels, and to of course confirm the reversal with an indication of higher than usual trading volume.

When you're looking at reversals, you want to ensure that you only trade in the extremes. The example you just saw was a stock that had made an extreme move to the downside before that move was reversed. A stock that has been selling off slowly all day long is usually not suitable for a reversal. That stock may be a good candidate for a Moving Average Trend trade (explained in the pages to come). You want to find stocks that are really stretched out to the downside or, for short selling, really stretched out to the upside, in a short period of time, and with high volume at the reversal point. You want to see that large extension, which means that you should look for considerable volume at the reversal point (such as the ALR Bottom Reversal in the above example from my scanner that is marked as Figure 7.13). Once you find that, you then must look for a couple of key indicators that will suggest that the price may be about to turn, and that is when you then take the position. I've said it many times: what goes up, must come down. Oftentimes these stocks will give up days' and weeks' or years' worth of price gain in just a matter of minutes. It is very critical to be able to correctly time the reversal.

I'll say it again: the key to your success with Top and Bottom Reversals is trading the extremes at or near a significant daily support or resistance level. How do I quantify these extremes? These are a few of the things that I look for:

1. An extreme RSI above 90 or below 10 will pique my interest.
2. A very high volume of shares being traded. Volume is usually increasing with the direction of price action and is at its maximum at the point of reversal.
3. Finally, more than five consecutive candles ending with an indecision candle or a Doji is definitely going to catch my attention. These candles usually demonstrate that sellers are losing their control while buyers are becoming more powerful, and that indicates the end of a trend. As you saw in the previous ALR example (Figures 7.12 and 7.13), sometimes reversals happen without an indecision candlestick. In those cases, you should look for strong reversal candlesticks – a bullish body for Bottom Reversals and a bearish body for Top Reversals.

I will add a caveat to this final point: there will be times when you will have between five and ten consecutive candles without much price action. They may be drifting down slowly, but not quickly enough for you to sense that it is a good reversal. You must look for a combination of these indicators all occurring at the same time. Never sell short just because the prices are too high. You should never argue with the crowd's decision, even if it doesn't make sense to you. You do not have to run with the crowd - but you should not run against it.

Utilizing all of these different factors will recreate the strategy that has been successful for me because of its attractive profit-to-loss ratio. Your profit-to-loss ratio is your average winners versus your average losers. Many new traders end up trading with a very poor profit-to-loss ratio because they sell their winners too soon and they hold their losers too long. This is an extremely common habit among new traders. The Reversal Strategy, however, lends itself to having a larger profit-to-loss ratio for new traders.

To summarize my trading strategy for the Bottom Reversal Strategy:

1. I set up a scanner to flag stocks with four or more consecutive candlesticks going downward in an extreme manner. When I see a stock hit my scanner, I quickly review the volume and daily levels of support or resistance near the stock to see if it will be a good candidate for a reversal trade or not.
2. I wait for confirmation of a Bottom Reversal Strategy: (1) formation of a bullish Doji or indecision candle or, instead, a very bullish candlestick, (2) the stock is being traded at or near a significant intraday support level, and (3) the RSI must be lower than 10.
3. When I see the stock make a new 1-minute or 5-minute high, I buy the stock.
4. My stop loss is the low of the previous red candlestick or the low of the day.
5. My profit target is either (1) the next level of support, or (2) VWAP (Volume Weighted Average Price, described later in this chapter) or 9 EMA or 20 EMA moving averages (whichever is closer), or (3) the stock makes a new 5-minute low, which means that the buyers are exhausted and the sellers are once again gaining control.

Top Reversal

As discussed before, a Top Reversal is similar to a Bottom Reversal, but on a short selling side. Let's take a look at Bed Bath & Beyond Inc. (ticker: BBBY) as it traded on June 23, 2016. My scanner, displayed in Figure 7.14 below, showed BBBY going up at 10:18 a.m. with six consecutive candles. It had a relative volume of almost 21.60, which meant it was trading significantly higher than usual (remember, we retail traders look for unusual trading volumes).

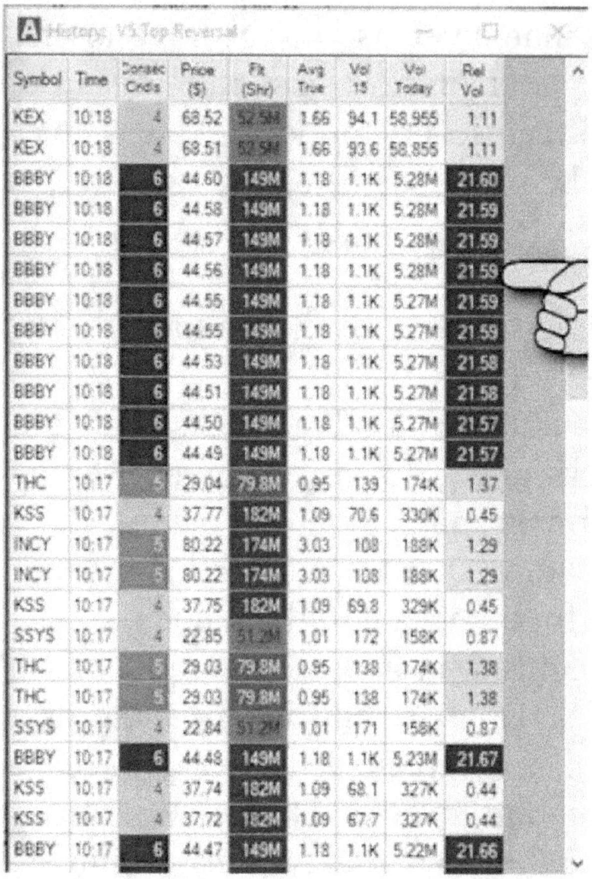

Symbol	Time	Consec Cndls	Price ($)	Fk (Shr)	Avg True	Vol 15	Vol Today	Rel Vol
KEX	10:18	4	68.52	52.5M	1.66	94.1	58,955	1.11
KEX	10:18	4	68.51	52.5M	1.66	93.6	58,855	1.11
BBBY	10:18	6	44.60	149M	1.18	1.1K	5.28M	21.60
BBBY	10:18	6	44.58	149M	1.18	1.1K	5.28M	21.59
BBBY	10:18	6	44.57	149M	1.18	1.1K	5.28M	21.59
BBBY	10:18	6	44.56	149M	1.18	1.1K	5.28M	21.59
BBBY	10:18	6	44.55	149M	1.18	1.1K	5.27M	21.59
BBBY	10:18	6	44.55	149M	1.18	1.1K	5.27M	21.59
BBBY	10:18	6	44.53	149M	1.18	1.1K	5.27M	21.58
BBBY	10:18	6	44.51	149M	1.18	1.1K	5.27M	21.58
BBBY	10:18	6	44.50	149M	1.18	1.1K	5.27M	21.57
BBBY	10:18	6	44.49	149M	1.18	1.1K	5.27M	21.57
THC	10:17	5	29.04	79.8M	0.95	139	174K	1.37
KSS	10:17	4	37.77	182M	1.09	70.6	330K	0.45
INCY	10:17	5	80.22	174M	3.03	108	188K	1.29
INCY	10:17	5	80.22	174M	3.03	108	188K	1.29
KSS	10:17	4	37.75	182M	1.09	69.8	329K	0.45
SSYS	10:17	4	22.85	51.2M	1.01	172	158K	0.87
THC	10:17	5	29.03	79.8M	0.95	138	174K	1.38
THC	10:17	5	29.03	79.8M	0.95	138	174K	1.38
SSYS	10:17	4	22.84	51.2M	1.01	171	158K	0.87
BBBY	10:17	6	44.48	149M	1.18	1.1K	5.23M	21.67
KSS	10:17	4	37.74	182M	1.09	68.1	327K	0.44
KSS	10:17	4	37.72	182M	1.09	67.7	327K	0.44
BBBY	10:17	6	44.47	149M	1.18	1.1K	5.22M	21.66

Figure 7.14 - Example of my Top Reversal real time scanner for BBBY.

I took this trade and made a good profit on it. I quickly reviewed the daily chart and found a significant resistance level at $44.40. I decided to see if I could get a good short entry near that level. A nice Doji around that level formed so I decided to take the trade. I shorted 800 shares at $44.10 when a new 5-minute candlestick was made, with my stop being the break of the high of the last 5-minute candlestick, which was also a new high of the day, as I have marked on Figure 7.15 below. I covered my shorts at VWAP near $43.10 for an $800 profit when the stock reached the VWAP.

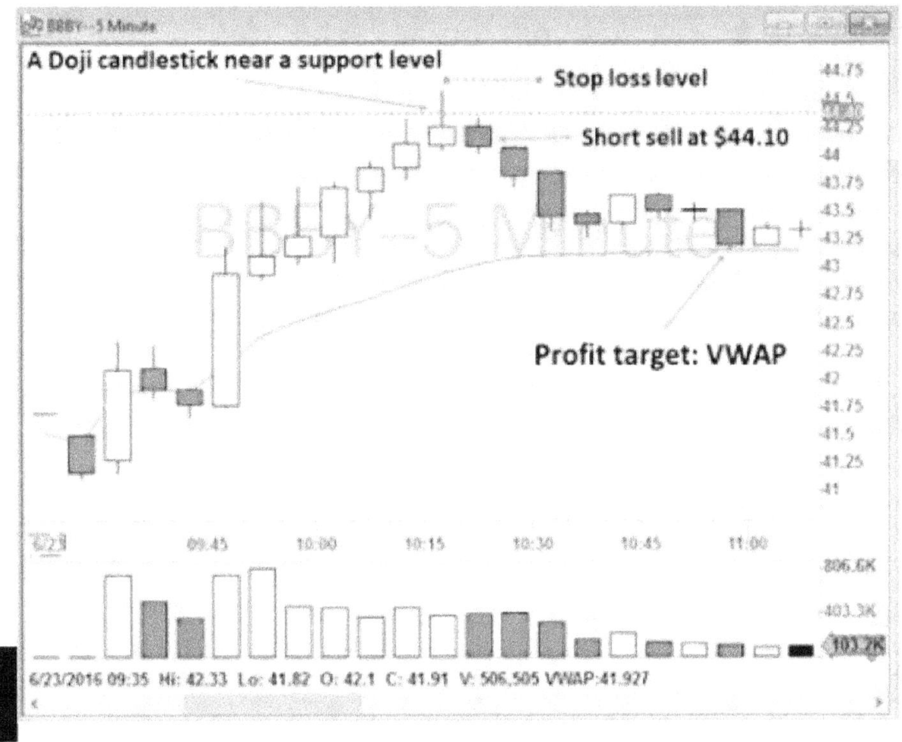

Figure 7.15 - Example of a Top Reversal Strategy on BBBY.

To summarize my trading strategy for the Top Reversal Strategy:

1. I set up a scanner to highlight stocks with four or more consecutive candlesticks moving upward. When I see the stock hit my scanner, I quickly review the volume and daily level of support or resistance near the stock to see if it will be a good trade or not.
2. I wait for confirmation of a Top Reversal Strategy: (1) formation of a bearish Doji or indecision candle or, instead, a very bearish candlestick, (2) the stock is being traded at or near a significant resistance level at high volume, and (3) the RSI must be higher than 90.
3. When I see the stock make a new 5-minute low, I consider this as a sign of weakness. I start short selling the stock if I have shares available to short.
4. My stop will be the high of the previous candlestick or simply the high of the day.
5. My profit target is either (1) the next level of support, or (2) VWAP or 9 EMA or 20 EMA moving averages (whichever is closer), or (3) when the stock makes a new 5-minute high, which means the buyers are once again gaining control and the sellers are exhausted.

Some day traders focus exclusively on reversal trades and in fact base their entire careers on them. Reversal trades are certainly the most classic of the various strategies with a very good risk/reward ratio and, interestingly, virtually every trading day you will find stocks that are good candidates for reversal trades. I myself am trading more and more reversal trades these days, especially during late morning and afternoon trading. However, reversal trading is not yet the cornerstone of my trading strategies. I am more of a VWAP and Support or Resistance trader, which I will explain later on in this book.

Strategy 5: Moving Average Trend Trading

Some traders use moving averages as potential entry and exit points for day trading. Many stocks will start an upside or downside trend after the morning session (around 11 a.m. New York time) and you will see their moving averages in 1-minute and 5-minute charts as a type of moving support or resistance line. Traders can benefit from this behavior and ride the trend along the moving average (on top of the moving average for going long or below the moving average for short selling).

As I explained in Chapter 5 about my indicators, I use 9 and 20 Exponential Moving Averages (EMA) and 50 and 200 Simple Moving Averages (SMA). For the sake of keeping this book short, I won't go into the details of what moving averages are and the differences between simple and exponential. You can, however, do a Google search and find detailed information about these moving averages or you can of course contact me directly through www.BearBullTraders.com with any questions you may have. I've also included very brief definitions in the glossary at the back of this book. Your charting software will have most of the moving averages built in. They are ready to be used and there is no need to change the default setting in them.

Let's take a look at the chart below, marked as Figure 7.16, for Direxion Daily Gold Miners Bull 3x Shrs ETF (ticker: NUGT) to see how you could trade based on 9 EMA on a 1-minute chart.

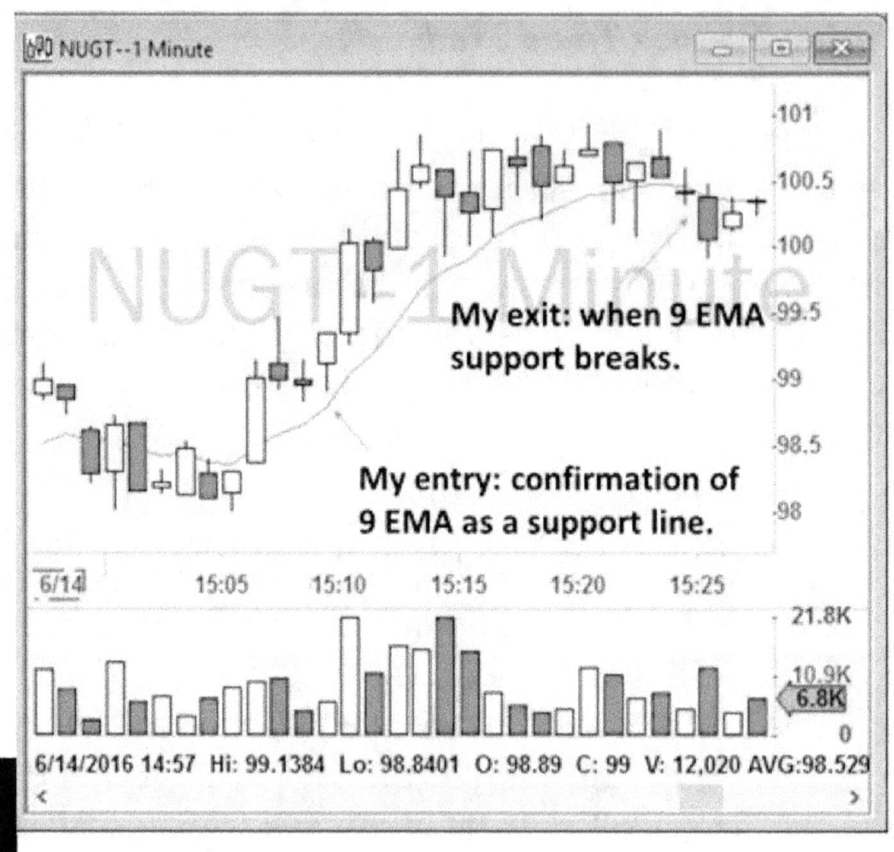

Figure 7.16 - Example of a long Moving Average Trend Strategy on NUGT on a 1-minute chart.

As you can see, at 15:06 p.m. I noticed NUGT had formed a Bull Flag. I saw that a consolidation period was happening on top of 9 EMA. As soon as I saw that 9 EMA was holding as the support, I jumped on the trade and rode the trend until the price broke the moving average at 15:21 p.m. I've marked my entry and exit points on the chart.

Moving Average Trends can happen in any intraday time frame. I monitor prices on both 1-minute and 5-minute charts and make my trades based only on these two time frames.

Let's take a look now at Figure 7.17, which is another Moving Average Trend on NUGT on June 16, 2016 on a 5-minute chart.

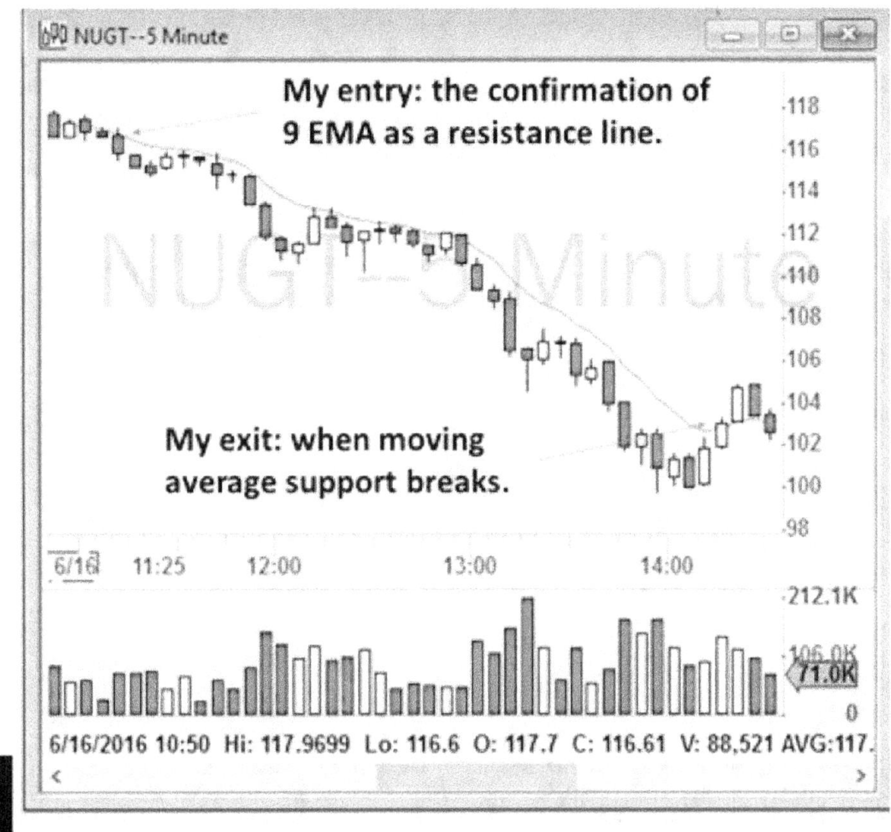

Figure 7.17 - Example of a short Moving Average Trend Strategy on NUGT on a 5-minute chart.

As you can see, NUGT sold off on a very steep downtrend from $116 to around $100: about a 14% drop in only two hours. I sold short early on the morning at around $115 with a stop loss at the break of 9 EMA on a 5-minute chart. I got stopped out at around 14:20 p.m. when the price broke the 9 EMA and closed above it at $104.

Let's take a look at another example, Celgene Corporation (CELG), on June 23, 2016. On the chart below, Figure 7.18, I've marked my entry and exit points and you will see how you can trade based on 9 EMA on a 5-minute chart. I entered the long position when 9 EMA held as a powerful support at around $99.90, and I then rode the upward move until 9 EMA broke at $100.40, for a profit of about 50 cents per share.

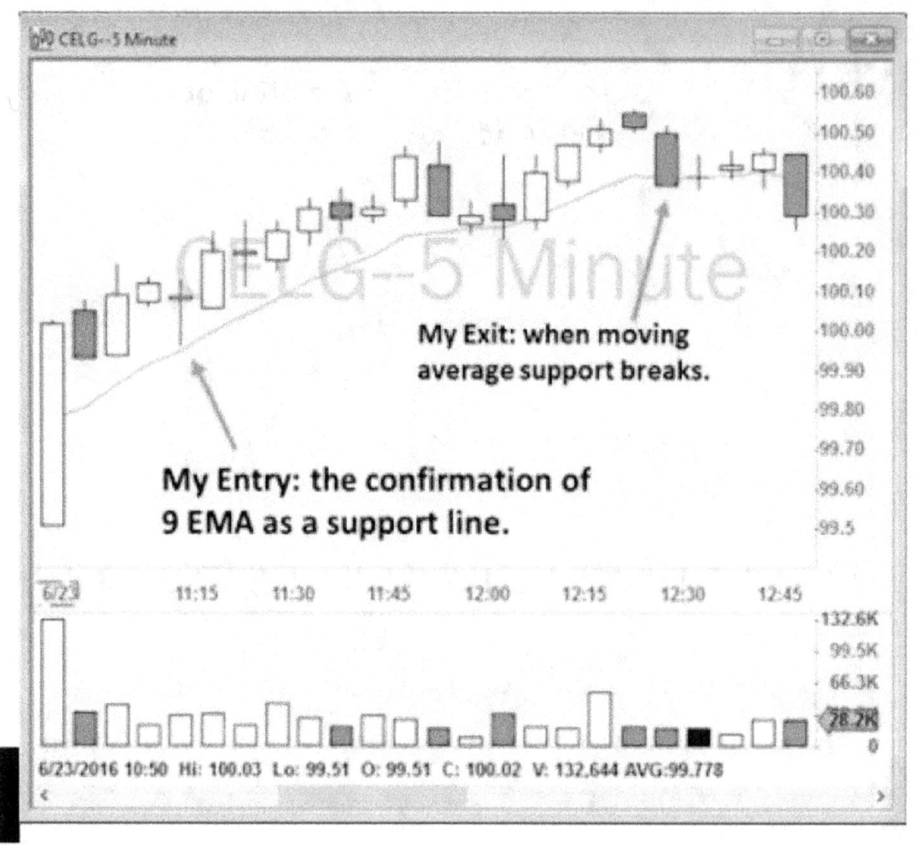

Figure 7.18 - Example of a Moving Average Trend Strategy on CELG.

Another example is Figure 7.19 below, a 5-minute chart for Exact Sciences Corp. (ticker: EXAS) on July 28, 2016 with 9 EMA.

Figure 7.19 - Example of a Moving Average Trend Strategy on EXAS.

Another fantastic example of a 9 EMA Moving Average Trend Strategy is set out below in Figure 7.20 for AMAG Pharmaceuticals, Inc. (ticker: AMAG). On January 9, 2017 its stock sold off from $31 to $23 in only a few hours. The 9 EMA held as a strong resistance. A great trade would have been a short sell on AMAG with a stop loss of the break of 9 EMA. In three areas marked on the chart, the price broke the 9 EMA and went slightly higher, but a 5-minute candlestick did not actually close above 9 EMA. These false breakouts usually happen with low volume. Experienced traders wait for a 5-minute candlestick to "close" above 9 EMA before they get out. A sudden break of 9 EMA with low volume may not be a good indicator of a trend coming to an end.

Figure 7.20 - Example of a Moving Average Trend Strategy on AMAG.

To summarize my trading strategy for Moving Average Trend trading:

1. When I am monitoring a Stock in Play and notice a trend is establishing around a moving average (usually 9 EMA), I consider trend trading. I quickly look at the previous days' trading data (on a 1-minute or 5-minute chart) to see if the stock is responding to these moving averages.
2. Once I learn which moving average is more suitable to the behavior

of the trade, I buy the stock after confirmation of moving averages as a support, and I buy as close as possible to the moving average line (in order to have a small stop). My stop will usually be 5 to 10 cents below the moving average line or, if a candlestick, close below the moving average (for long positions). For short positions, a close above moving average would stop me out.

3. I ride the trend until the break of moving average.
4. I never use trailing stops and I constantly monitor the trend with my eyes.
5. If the stock is moving really high away from the moving average, offering me an equally really nice unrealized profit, I may take some profit, usually at half-position. I do not always wait until the break of moving average for my exit. Traders say: you can never go broke by taking good profits. If the price pulls back to the moving average, I may add again to my position and continue the trend trade.

I personally don't trade very often based on moving averages. I look at them to see potential levels of support or resistance, but I rarely make any trade based upon a trend because, in a trend trade strategy, you are usually left exposed in the market for a considerable length of time. Some trend trades can last as long as several hours and that is too long for my personality. I would like to take my profit in a matter of minutes. I rarely will wait even an hour. Another reason that I do not often trade these strategies is that they usually best work during Mid-day and the Close. At the Open (in the morning session), when volatility is high, it's hard to identify a Moving Average Trend play. These slow trends are best identified during Mid-day, when there is low volatility, and they usually end near the Close (around 3 p.m. New York time) when the professional traders on Wall Street start to dominate the trading.

Having said that, a Moving Average Trend Strategy is an excellent trading strategy, because it usually does not require a very fast decision making process and trade execution. It also often does not require the use of Hotkeys. You can enter the trades manually and still be successful. In addition, entry points and your stop loss can be clearly recognized from the moving averages on the charts. This is especially important for traders who pay high retail commissions (sometimes as high as $4.95/trade) and cannot scale in and out of trades without a high fee. The Moving Average Trend Strategy has clear entry and exit points and usually a good profit can be made by only two orders, one for entry and one for the exit.

As I have discussed, strategies depend on your account size, personality, psychology of trading and risk tolerance, as well as on your software and the tools and brokers that you have. The combination of all of these factors have led me to be a VWAP trader who sometimes trades with the Opening Range Breakout Strategy. I also often trade Support or Resistance Strategies, which I will explain further in the next sections. However, I want to emphasize that trading strategies are not something that you can imitate just from reading a book, speaking with a mentor, or attending a class. You have to slowly and methodically develop your preferred method and then stick with it. There is nothing wrong with any strategy if it works for you. There is no good and bad in any of these strategies; it truly is a matter of personal choice.

Strategy 6: VWAP Trading

Volume Weighted Average Price, or VWAP, is the most important technical indicator for day traders. Definitions of VWAP can be found in both Wikipedia and many other online resources. I will skip explaining it in detail for the sake of keeping this guide short, but essentially, VWAP is a moving average that takes into account the volumes of the shares being traded at any price. Other moving averages are calculated based only on the price of the stock on the chart, but VWAP also considers the number of shares in that stock that are being traded on every price. Your trading platform should have VWAP built into it and you can use it without changing any of its default settings.

VWAP is an indicator of who is in control of the price action - the buyers or the sellers. When stock is traded above the VWAP, it means that the buyers are in overall control of the price and there is a buying demand on the stock. When a stock price breaks below the VWAP, it is safe to assume that the sellers are gaining control over the price action.

VWAP is often used to measure the trading efficiency of institutional traders. Professional traders working for investment banks or hedge funds who need to trade large amount of shares each day cannot enter or exit the market by just one single order. The market is not liquid enough to enter a one-million share buy order. Therefore, they need to liquidate their orders slowly during the day. After buying or selling a large position in a stock during the day, institutional traders compare their price to VWAP values. A buy order executed below the VWAP would be considered a good fill for them because the stock was bought at a below average price (meaning that the trader has bought their large position at a relatively discounted price compared to the market). Conversely, a sell order executed above the VWAP would be deemed a good fill because it was sold at an above average price. Therefore, VWAP is used by institutional traders to identify good entry and exit points. Institutional traders with large orders try to buy or sell large positions around VWAP. The performance of institutional traders is often evaluated based on what price they fill their large orders at. Traders who buy significantly higher than VWAP may be penalized because they cost the institution money for taking that large position. Institutional traders therefore try to buy below or as close to VWAP as possible. Conversely, when a professional trader has to get rid of a large position, they try to sell at the VWAP or higher. Day traders who know this may benefit from this market activity.

After the market opens, the Stock in Play will trade heavily in the first five minutes. If the Stock in Play has gapped up, some individual shareholders, hedge funds or investment banks may want to as soon as possible sell their shares for a profit, before the price drops. At the same time, some investors wanting to take positions in the stock want to buy as soon as possible before the price goes even higher. Therefore, in the first five minutes, an unknown heavy trading is happening between the overnight shareholders and the new investors. Scalpers usually ride the momentum right at the Open. After volatility decreases around ten to fifteen minutes into the Open, the stock will move toward or away from the VWAP. This is a test to see if there is a large investment bank waiting to buy or sell. If there is a large institutional trader aiming to buy a significant position, the stock will pop over the VWAP and move even higher. This is a good opportunity for us day traders to go long.

Conversely, if there are large shareholders wanting to get rid of their shares, then this is a good point for them to liquidate their positions. They start selling their shares at the VWAP. The price will reject the VWAP and start to move down. This is an excellent short selling opportunity for day traders. If there is no interest in the stock from market makers or institutions, the price may trade sideways near VWAP. Wise traders will then stay away from that stock.

Trading based on VWAP can be very easy for beginner traders to master because so many traders study the VWAP and make decisions based on it. Therefore, a beginner trader can easily be on the right side of the trade. When a stock tries to break the VWAP but cannot, you can short the stock because you can safely assume that the other traders that are watching will also begin to short. A trading strategy based on VWAP is a simple and easy strategy to follow. I usually short stocks when traders try but fail to break the VWAP on 5-minute charts.

Let's have a look now at Figure 7.21 which documents a trade that I took on SolarCity Corporation (ticker: SCTY) on June 24, 2016.

Figure 7.21 - Example of a long VWAP Strategy on SCTY.

At around 10:30 a.m. on June 24, 2016, I noticed that SCTY had found a support above VWAP at around $21. I purchased 1,000 shares of the stock with the anticipation of moving toward $22 with VWAP as a support. My stop was a 5-minute candlestick close below VWAP. I first sold a half-size position at $21.50, and then moved my stop to break-even. I sold another position at $22 because I know half-dollars (such as $1.50, $2.50, $3.50) and whole dollars ($1, $2, $3) usually act at a support or resistance level.

VWAP also works well when you want to short stocks. Let's have a look at Figure 7.22, which documents another trade that I took on SCTY, this time on June 22, 2016, and this time on the short side.

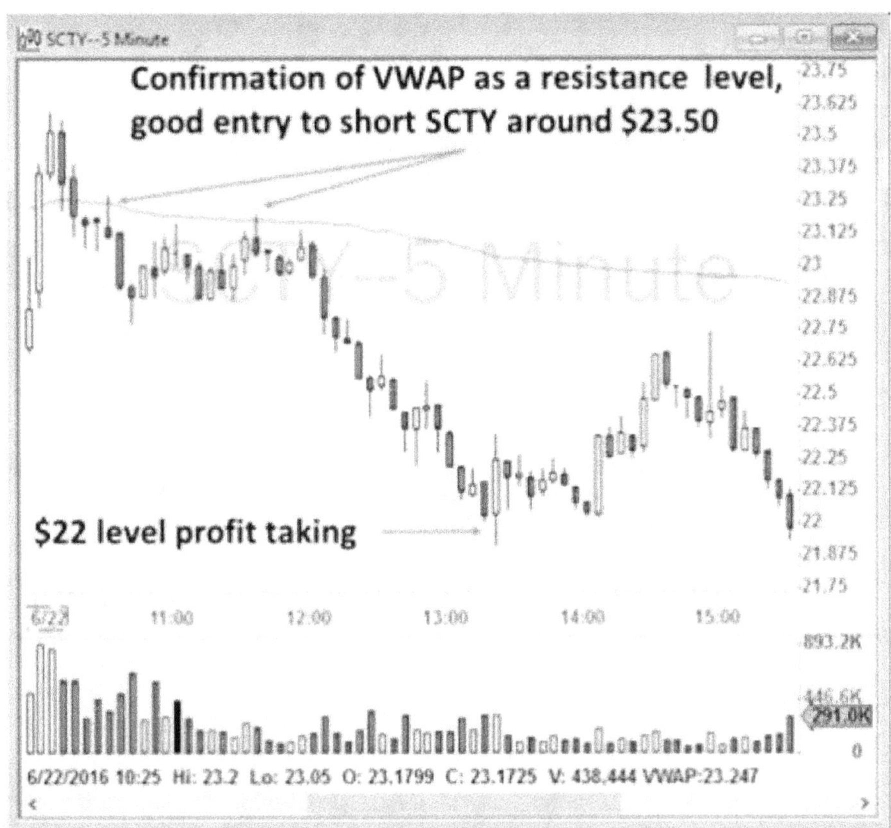

Figure 7.22 - Example of a short VWAP Strategy on SCTY.

At around 11 a.m., I noticed that SCTY had faced a resistance over VWAP. I shorted the stock with the anticipation of losing the VWAP at around $23. At around 12 p.m., the buyers gave up and the sellers took control of the price action. I had a nice run down to $22 and covered my shorts at $22 for a good $1,000 profit.

To summarize my trading strategy for VWAP trading:

1. When I make my watchlist for the day, I monitor the price action around VWAP at the Open. If a stock shows respect toward VWAP, then I wait until a confirmation of the VWAP break (for short selling) or VWAP support (for going long).
2. I usually buy as close as possible to VWAP to minimize my risk. My stop will be a break and a close 5-minute close below VWAP. For short selling, I short near VWAP with a stop loss of a close above the VWAP.
3. I keep the trade until I hit my profit target or until I reach a new support or resistance level.
4. I usually sell half-positions near the profit target or support or resistance level and move my stop up to my entry point or break-

even.

Strategy 7: Support or Resistance Trading

Many traders love to draw diagonal trend lines. But after making thousands of trades, I've come to the conclusion that the market doesn't know diagonal price levels. In my opinion, diagonal trend lines are subjective, and can result from wishful thinking. You can draw a trend line across any prices or zones in a way that can change its slope and its message. If you're in a mood to buy, you can draw your trend line a little steeper. If you feel like shorting, you'll "recognize" a downtrend. None of those diagonal trend lines are objective, and I am skeptical of them. The biggest pitfall with this kind of trend line charting is wishful thinking. Traders will find themselves identifying bullish or bearish trends depending on whether they're in a mood to buy or sell.

Horizontal support or resistance trading is my favorite style of trading. My years of experience have taught me that the market only remembers price levels, which is why horizontal support or resistance lines make sense, but diagonal trend lines are subjective and open to self-deception. In fact, trend lines are among the most deceptive of all tools in trading. I therefore avoid trend lines.

Support is a price level where buying is strong enough to interrupt or reverse a downtrend. When a downtrend hits a support level, it bounces. Support is represented on a chart by a horizontal line connecting two or more bottoms (see Figure 7.23 below).

Resistance is a price level where selling is strong enough to interrupt or reverse an uptrend. When an uptrend hits a resistance level, it acts like a person who hits their head on a ceiling while climbing a ladder - they stop and might even tumble down. Resistance is represented on a chart by a horizontal line connecting two or more tops (as also set out in Figure 7.23 below).

Minor support or resistance causes trends to pause, while major support or resistance causes them to reverse. Traders buy at support and sell at resistance, making their effectiveness a self-fulfilling prophecy.

Using this method, every morning I shortlist the stocks that I would like to trade based on the criteria I set forth in Chapter 4: a stock that has fundamental catalysts such as news, an extreme earnings report or a new drug approval. These Stocks in Play are the ones that retail traders are watching and planning to trade.

Before the market opens, I go back to the daily charts and find price levels that have been shown in the past to be critical. Finding price support or resistance levels is tricky and requires trading experience. If you watch me trading every morning, you will see how I place my support or resistance lines on my Stocks in Play.

For example, let's take a look at Figure 7.23, a SCTY daily chart without support or resistance lines and another including the lines.

Figure 7.23 - Example of a Support or Resistance Strategy on SCTY daily chart.

Support or resistance lines on daily charts are not always easy to find, and at times you will not be able to draw anything clear. If I cannot see anything clear, I don't have to draw anything. There is a good chance that other traders will also not see those lines clearly and therefore there is no point in forcing myself to draw support or resistance lines. In that case, I will plan my trades based on the VWAP or Moving Averages or other chart patterns that I earlier discussed.

Here are some hints for drawing support or resistance lines on daily charts:

1. You will usually see indecision candles in the area of support or resistance because that is where buyers and sellers are closely fighting each other.
2. Half-dollars and whole dollars usually act at a support or resistance level, especially in lower than $10 stocks. If you don't find a support or resistance line around these numbers on daily charts, remember that in day trading these numbers can act as an invisible support or resistance line.
3. You should always look at the recent data to draw lines.
4. The more of a line that is touching extreme price lines, the more that the line is a better support or resistance and has more value. Give that line more emphasis.
5. Only the support or resistance lines in the current price range are

important. If the price of the stock is currently $20, there is no point in finding support or resistance lines in the region when it was $40. It is unlikely that the stock will move and reach that area. Find only the support or resistance area that is close to your day trading range.

6. Support or resistance lines are actually an "area" and not exact numbers. For example, when you find an area around $19.69 as a support line, you must expect price action movement around that number but not at exactly $19.69. Depending on the price of the stock, an area of 5 to 10 cents is safe to assume. In the example with a support line of $19.69, the real support area might range from $19.62 to $19.72.

7. The price must have a clear bounce from that level. If you are not certain if the price has bounced in that level, then it is probably not a support or resistance level. Important support or resistance levels on daily charts stand out. They shout at you: "grab me by the face".

8. For day trading, it is better to draw support or resistance lines across the extreme prices or wicks on daily levels rather than across areas where the bulk of the bars stopped. This is the complete opposite of swing trading. For swing trading, you need to draw support or resistance lines across the edges of congested areas where the bulk of the bars stopped rather than across the extreme prices. This is because the close price is more important for swing trading than the extreme wicks in daily bars are. The close price of a stock on a daily chart is the price that the market makers and professional traders have agreed on. Previous extreme high and low wicks have been made by day traders, so you should look at those.

Placing support or resistance lines, although tricky, is actually quite simple once you get the hang of it. Please feel free to watch me every morning in our chatroom when I place my support and resistance levels. As I've mentioned, I share my platform live with our trading community.

Let's review a trade that I took based on these lines. Please see Figures 7.24 to 7.26 below. CarMax (ticker: KMX), the United States' largest used-car retailer, on June 21, 2016 had extreme earnings and its stock gapped down over 3%. That was a perfect opportunity for retail traders like us to find a good trade plan. I quickly found the support or resistance area level on a daily chart and watched the price action around those levels.

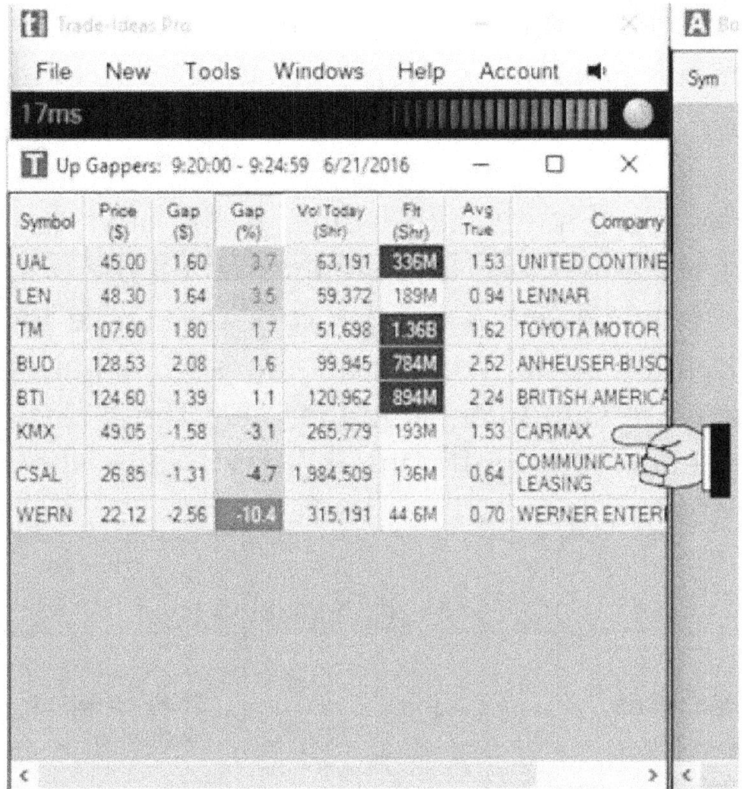

Figure 7.24 - My Gappers watchlist on June 21, 2016 at 9:20 a.m. showing KMX may be a Stock in Play for that day.

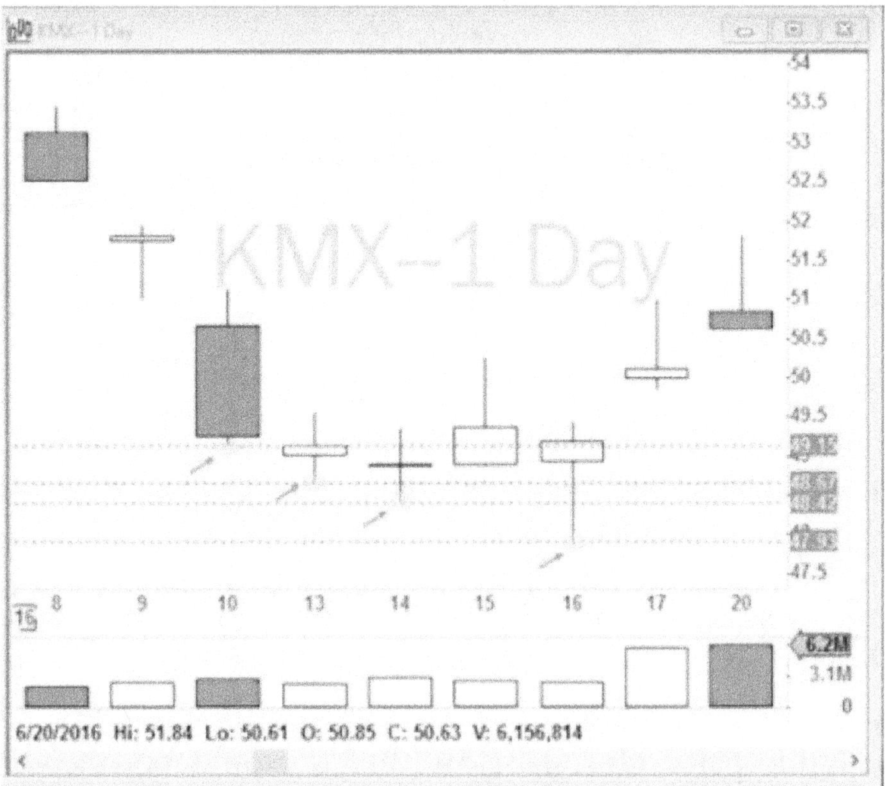

Figure 7.25 - KMX support or resistance lines on a daily chart up to June 20, 2016.

After reviewing the daily charts up to June 20, 2016, I found four levels of $47.93, $48.42, $48.67, and $49.15. As you can see in Figure 7.25 above, all of these levels are extreme price levels for the previous days and, as I explained, I give more attention to wicks and extreme prices than I do to the open or close prices.

Now, let's take a look at Figure 7.26, which is the next day intraday chart for June 21, 2016, and see how those levels appeared on the price action. I marked the areas that those levels acted as a support or resistance level. Do ensure that you give special attention to the volume of shares traded at or near those levels. Do you see that they are significantly higher near those levels? A high volume confirms that these levels are significant and day traders should pay attention to them.

Figure 7.26 - Example of a Support or Resistance Strategy on KMX on a 5-minute chart with my trades for that day.

When the market opened, I watched the stock and realized that the area of around $48.67 acted as a resistance level at the Open. Later, the stock sold off to $47.93 with high volume. I bought 1,000 shares at that support, with a stop loss below $47.93. If the price closed below that, I would be out with a loss. The price instead quickly bounced back, just like a diver hitting the bottom of the ocean. I sold 500 shares at $48.42 for a nice $500 profit. I sold the other 500 shares at the next resistance level of $48.67 for a nice $750 profit. I kept monitoring the price action and, later in the afternoon, when the price rejected the $49.15 level with high volume, I went short with a stop loss of a new high of the day or a close above $49.15. I covered half of my shares at the level of $48.67 and the other half at $48.42, both for another nice profit.

To summarize my trading strategy for support or resistance trading:

1. Each morning, after I make my watchlist for the day, I quickly look at the daily charts for that watchlist and find the areas of support or resistance.
2. I monitor the price action around those areas on a 5-minute chart. If an indecision candle forms around that area, that is the confirmation of that level and I enter the trade. I usually buy as close as possible to the support level to minimize my risk. Stop will be a break and a close of a 5-minute candlestick under the support level.
3. I will take profit near the next support or resistance level.
4. I keep the trade open until I hit my profit target or I reach a new support or resistance level.
5. I usually sell half-positions near the profit target or support or resistance level and move my stop up to my entry point for break-even.
6. If there are no next obvious support or resistance levels, I will consider closing my trade at or near half-dollar or round-dollar levels.

A similar approach will also work when you sell short a stock below a resistance level.

Strategy 8: Red-to-Green Trading

Red-to-Green is another easy to recognize trading strategy. As I mentioned in Chapter 5, one of the indicators I have on my chart is the *previous day close* level. The previous day close is a powerful level of support or resistance and traders should trade toward it when there is rising volume.

If the current price of a stock is higher than the previous day close (for Stocks in Play that gapped up), the market is moving from a Green day to a Red day (meaning that the percentage that the price has changed will now be negative, which will be shown as red in most of the Exchanges and platforms). This is a Green-to-Red move.

If the price is lower than the previous day close (for stocks that gapped down), the market is moving from a Red day to a Green day (meaning that the percentage that the price has changed will now be positive, which will be shown as green in most of the Exchanges and platforms). This is a Red-to-Green move.

The strategy is almost identical for both Red-to-Green and Green-to-Red except for the direction of the trade (short or long). So, for the sake of simplicity, I will use the term Red-to-Green Strategy for both directions, but depending on the trade, I may be referring to a Green-to-Red trade.

For example, take a look at Figure 7.27, the 5-minute chart for Mallinckrodt Public Limited Company (ticker: MNK), which was a Stock in Play on January 19, 2017. After a weak Open, the price held below VWAP. I went short, but there was no nearby support or resistance level except the previous day close at $46.52 (the dashed line on my chart). Therefore, I decided to go short from VWAP at around $47.80 for the profit target of the previous day close at $46.52, a nice $1.20 per share profit.

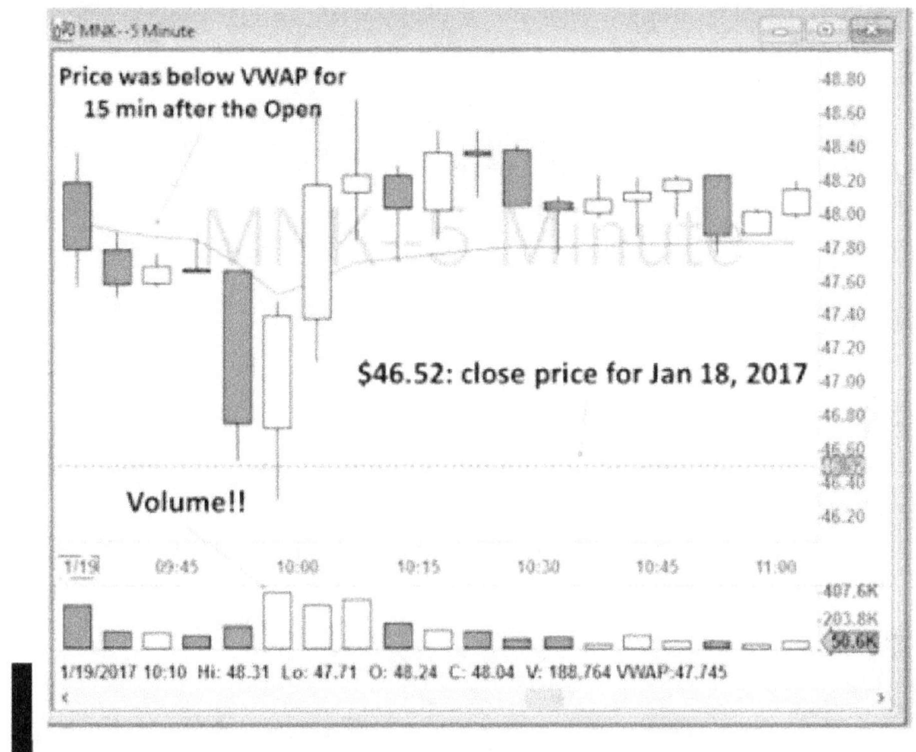

Figure 7.27 - Example of a short sell Red-to-Green Strategy on MNK.

For another example, let's take a look at Figure 7.28, the 5-minute chart for Barracuda Networks, Inc. (ticker: CUDA) on January 10, 2017. The same price action can be seen at the Open. CUDA gapped up in the pre-market because of a good earnings report. At the Open, it was sold off heavily, perhaps because overnight shareholders and long-term investors started to sell their shares for a profit. The stock tested the VWAP for about twenty minutes and then sold off in a high volume toward the previous day close of $23.81. Its price bounced back later, during Mid-day, toward the VWAP, after it could not break the previous day close. Later, in the early afternoon, the price sold off again toward the previous day close for another Red-to-Green trade before it bounced back yet again.

In this example too, the previous day close level of $23.81 acted as a strong support level. In both morning and afternoon trading, a short sell opportunity was possible from VWAP at around $24.40 to $23.81. I did not take this trade as I was trading another stock around the same time that day.

Figure 7.28 - Example of a short Red-to-Green Strategy on CUDA.

To summarize my trading strategy for Red-to-Green trading:

1. When I make my watchlist for the day, I monitor the price action around the previous day close.
2. If a stock moves toward the previous day close with high volume, I consider going long with the profit target of the previous day close.
3. My stop loss is the nearest technical level. If I buy near VWAP, my stop loss will be the break of VWAP. If I buy near a moving average or an important support level, my stop loss will be the break of moving average or support level.
4. I usually sell all at the profit target. If the price moves in my favor, I bring my stop loss to the break-even and do not let the price turn against me. Red-to-Green moves should work immediately.

A similar approach will work equally as well when you short a stock for a Green-to-Red Strategy (see the MNK and CUDA examples in Figures 7.27 and 7.28 above).

Strategy 9: Opening Range Breakouts

Another well-known trading strategy is the so-called Opening Range Breakout (ORB). This strategy signals an entry point, but does not determine the profit target. You should define the best profit target based on the other technical levels you learn from this book. Later on, you will notice that I list further possible profit targets. The ORB is an entry signal only, but remember, a full trading strategy must define the proper entry, exit and stop loss.

Right at the market Open (9:30 a.m. New York time), Stocks in Play usually experience violent price action that arises from heavy buy and sell orders that come into the market. This heavy trading in the first five minutes is the result of the profit or loss taking of the overnight position holders as well as new investors and traders. If a stock has gapped up, some overnight traders start selling their position for a profit. At the same time, some new investors might jump in to buy the stock before the price goes higher. If a stock gaps down, on the other hand, some investors might panic and dump their shares right at the Open before it drops any lower. On the other side, some institutions might think this drop could be a good buying opportunity and they will start buying large positions at a discounted price.

Therefore, there is a complicated mass psychology unfolding at the Open for the Stocks in Play. Wise traders sit on their hands and watch for the opening ranges to develop and allow the other traders to fight against each other until one side wins.

Typically, you want to give the opening range at least five minutes. This is called the 5-minute Opening Range Breakout (ORB). Some traders will wait even longer, such as for thirty minutes or even for one hour, to identify the balance of the power between the buyers and sellers. They then develop a trade plan in the direction of the 30-minute or 60-minute breakout. In the past, I only traded the trade at the 5-minute ORB, but recently I am more in favor of the 15-minute ORB or the 30-minute ORB. The longer the time frame, the less volatility you can expect compared to the 5-minute range. As with most setups, the ORB Strategy tends to work best with mid to large cap stocks, which do not show wild price swings intraday. I do not recommend trading this strategy with low float stocks that have gapped up or down. Ideally, the stock should trade within a range which is smaller than the Average True Range of the stock (ATR). The upper and lower boundaries of the range can be identified by the high and low of the 5-, 15-, 30-or 60-minute candlesticks.

To gain a better understanding of this strategy, let’s take a look at Figures 7.29 and 7.30 for e.l.f. Beauty Inc. (ticker: ELF) on March 9, 2017. ELF was on my Gappers watchlist that day, and had gapped up over 19% for good results. I decided to watch it closely to see if I could trade it on the short side. There was a good chance that many overnight investors and traders would try to sell their positions for profit. An overnight profit of 19% is very tempting for many investors. Why not take the profit?

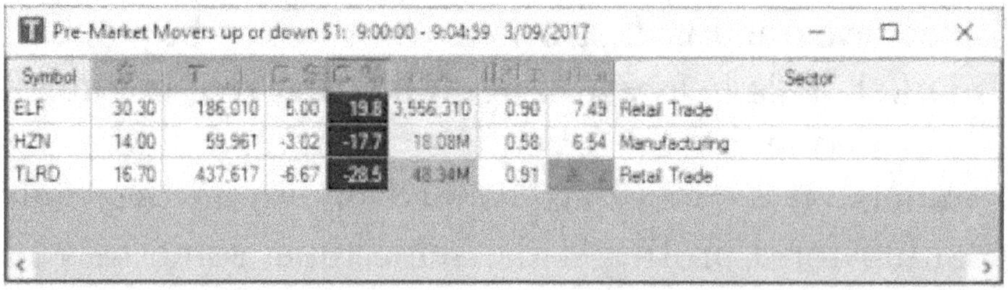
Pre-Market Movers up or down $1: 9:00:00 - 9:04:59 3/09/2017

Symbol								Sector
ELF	30.30	186.010	5.00	19.8	3,556.310	0.90	7.49	Retail Trade
HZN	14.00	59.961	-3.02	-17.7	18.08M	0.58	6.54	Manufacturing
TLRD	16.70	437.617	-6.67	-28.5	48.34M	0.91	[illegible]	Retail Trade

Figure 7.29 - My Gappers watchlist on March 9, 2017 at 9 a.m. showing ELF may be a Stock in Play for that day.

As you can see in Figure 7.30 below, the stock opened at $31 and sold off heavily to below $30 in the first five minutes. That was the sign that investors were selling for profit after it had gapped up 19%. I waited for the first 5-minute battle of buyers and sellers to settle down. As soon as I saw that the price broke the 5-minute opening range, I went short below VWAP. As I mentioned before, ORB is a buy or sell signal, and you must define the proper exit and stop loss for it. For me, stop loss is always a close above VWAP for short positions, and a break below VWAP for long positions. Profit target point is the next important technical level.

As you can also see in Figure 7.30 below, I rode the wave down to the next daily level of $28.62 and covered my shorts at around that level.

Figure 7.30 - Example of the Opening Range Breakout Strategy on ELF 5-minute chart.

Another example could be Procter & Gamble Co. (ticker: PG) on February 15, 2017. The stock hit my Gappers scanner, see Figure 7.31, and I had it on my watchlist at the Open.

Pre-Market Movers up or down $1: 9:00:00 - 9:04:59 2/15/2017

Symbol	$	T	C	G				Sector
SODA	50.70	107,445	3.35	7.1	20.93M	1.04	5.78	Manufacturing
PG	89.44	449,389	1.58	1.8	2.56B	0.79	1.37	Manufacturing
AIG	63.10	552,600	-3.79	-6.7	1.03B	0.81	1.45	Finance and Insurance
FOSL	18.71	702,161	-4.16	-18.2	33.85M	1.11	35.88	Wholesale Trade

Figure 7.31 - My Gappers watchlist on February 15, 2017 at 9 a.m. showing PG may be a Stock in Play for that day.

As you can see below in Figure 7.32, in only the first five minutes more than 2.6 million shares were traded, but PG's price only moved from $89.89 to $89.94; a range of only 5 cents while the Average True Range (ATR) of PG was $0.79. As I have mentioned, you need the opening range to be smaller than the daily ATR. If a stock moves near or higher than its ATR at the Open, it is not a good candidate for the ORB Strategy. It means that the stock is too volatile and without a catchable move. It is worth mentioning again, Stocks in Play move, and those moves are directional and catchable. If a stock constantly moves up and down $2 with high volume, but without any directional signal, you want to stay away from it. Those stocks are usually being heavily traded by computers.

In the PG example, as soon as I saw that it broke the opening range to the upside, I went long and rode the wave up toward the next resistance level of $91.01. If there was no obvious technical level for the exit and profit target, you can exit when a stock shows signs of weakness. For example, if its price makes a new 5-minute low, that means weakness, and you should consider selling if you are long. If you are short and if the stock makes a new 5-minute high, then it could be a sign of strength and you may want to cover your short position. In this PG example, if you did not previously identify the $91.01 level, you could exit when PG made a new 5-minute low just below $91. I marked it for you on Figure 7.32 below.

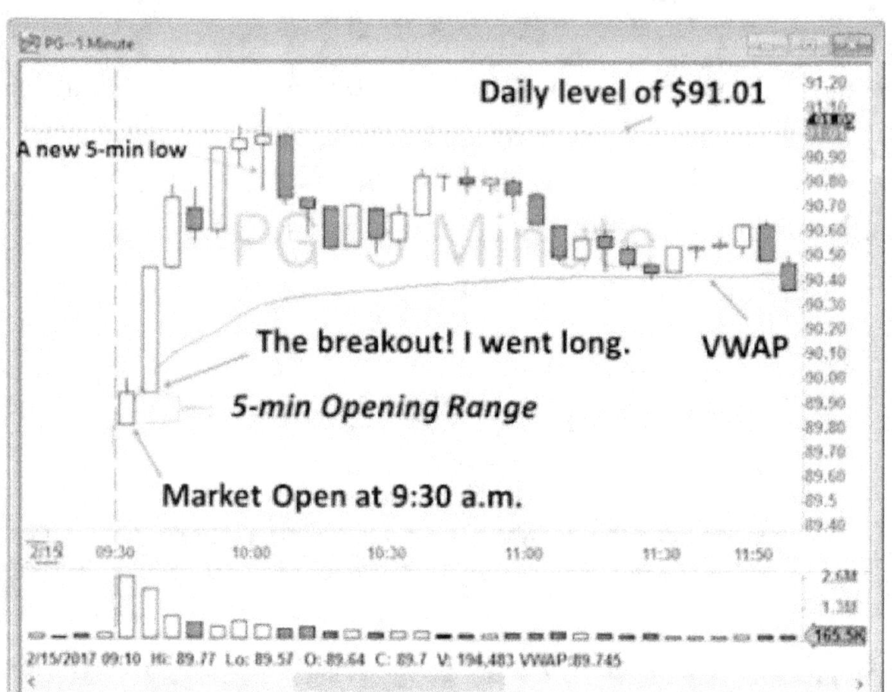

Figure 7.32 - Example of the Opening Range Breakout Strategy on PG daily chart.

To summarize my Opening Range Breakout Strategy:

1. After I build my watchlist in the morning, I closely monitor the shortlisted stocks in the first five minutes. I identify their opening range and their price action. How many shares are being traded? Is the stock jumping up and down or does it have a directional upward or downward movement? Is it high volume with large orders only, or are there many orders going through? I prefer stocks that have high volume, but also with numerous different orders being traded.

A stock that has traded 1 million shares, but those shares were only ten orders of 100,000 shares each, is not a liquid stock to trade. Volume alone does not show the liquidity; the number of orders being sent to the Exchange is as important.

2. The opening range must be significantly smaller than the stock's Average True Range (ATR). I have ATR as a column in my Trade Ideas scanner.

3. After the close of the first five minutes of trading, the stock may continue to be traded in that opening range in the next five minutes. But, if I see the stock is breaking the opening range, I enter the trade according to the direction of the breakout: long for an upward breakout and short for a downward move.

4. My stop loss is a close below VWAP for the long positions and a break above VWAP for the short positions.

5. My profit target is the next important technical level, such as: (1) important intraday daily levels that I identify in the pre-market, (2) moving averages on a daily chart, and/or (3) previous day close.

6. If there was no obvious technical level for the exit and profit target, I exit when a stock shows signs of weakness (if I am long) or strength (if I am short). For example, if the price makes a new 5-minute low, that means weakness and I consider selling my position if I am long. If I am short and the stock makes a new 5-minute high, then it could be a sign of strength and I consider covering my short position.

My strategy above was for a 5-minute ORB, but the same process will also work well for 15-minute or 30-minute opening range breakouts.

Other Trading Strategies

You have now read a summary of my trading strategies. You may be wondering what other traders do. As I mentioned before, there are unlimited numbers of trading strategies that individuals have developed for themselves. Traders often choose and modify their strategies based on personal factors such as account size, amount of time that can be dedicated to trading, trading experience, personality and risk tolerance.

You should develop your own strategy. A trading strategy is very personalized to each individual. My risk tolerance and psychology are most likely different from yours and from those of other traders. I might not be comfortable with a $500 loss, but someone who has a large account can easily hold onto the loss and eventually make profit out of a losing trade. You cannot mirror-trade anyone else; you must develop your own risk management method and strategy.

Some traders focus heavily on technical indicators like the RSI, the moving average convergence divergence (also known as the MACD), or the moving average crossover. There are hundreds, if not thousands, of sophisticated technical indicators out there. Some traders believe they have found the Holy Grail of technical indicators, and it might be a combination of RSI or the moving average crossover. I don't believe having a large number of technical indicators will automatically make you a successful day trader. Day trading is not mechanical and automated; it is discretionary: traders need to make real time decisions. The success of each strategy is based on judgment and the proper execution of it by the trader.

I am also skeptical of the strategies that have many indicators. I don't think that having more indicators on your chart helps you in day trading, especially since you need to be able to process information very quickly, at times in just a matter of seconds. I have found that often indicators' signals will also contradict each other and that will lead to confusion.

That is why my day trading indicators are limited to VWAP and a few other moving averages. For my swing trading, I use more complicated indicators such as MACD because I do not have to make quick decisions. I usually review my swing trading after the market closes, with proper due diligence and evaluation. You can easily find more information about the indicators I've mentioned in this section, along with many others, by doing a simple online search.

Some of my day trader colleagues may disagree with me, but as I mentioned above, my personal experience is that you cannot enter a trade with a mechanical and systematic approach and then let the indicators dictate your entry and exit. That is my next rule: **Rule 10:** Indicators only indicate; they should not be allowed to dictate.

Computers are trading all of the time. When you set up a system for trading that has no input or requires no decisions by the trader, then you are entering the world of algorithmic trading, and you will lose trades to investment banks that have million-dollar algorithms and billions of dollars in cash for trading.

Of course, I use the RSI in my scanner for some of my trading strategies, and in particular for reversal trading. Obviously, I have scanners that rely on a high or low RSI, but those are more conditioned to find stocks at extremes. They are by no means a buy or sell indicator.

Develop Your Own Strategy

You must still find your own place in the market. I may be a 1-minute or a 5-minute trader; you may be a 60-minute trader. Some may be daily or weekly traders (swing traders). There's a place in the market for everyone. Consider what you are learning in this book as pieces of a puzzle that together make up the bigger picture of your trading career. You're going to acquire some pieces here, you're going to pick up pieces on your own from your own reading and research, and, overall, you will create a puzzle that will develop into your own unique trading strategy. I don't expect everything I do to work exactly the same for you. I am happy to help you develop a strategy that is going to work for you, your personality, your account size and your risk tolerance. Please contact me in our chatroom at www.BearBullTraders.com.

The key for now is that you master one strategy. Once you can tread water in the market with your one strategy, you can be a trader without blowing up your account. This is simply a matter of spending time in the chair. The more time you spend watching your charts, the more you will learn. This is a job where you survive until you can make it. You can start casting out later, but first you need to master just one strategy. It can be the VWAP trade, it can be a Support or Resistance Strategy, it can be a Reversal Strategy, or you can create a strategy of your own. Narrow the choices down, develop that area of strength into a workable strategy, and then use that strategy to survive until you are able to develop others.

It is absolutely critical for every trader to be trading a strategy. Plan a trade, and trade the plan. I wish someone had said to me when I first started training, *"Andrew, you need to trade a strategy. If you're trading with real money, you must be trading a written strategy, and it must have historical data to verify that it's worth trading with real money."* You cannot change your plan once you have already entered the trade and have an open position.

The truth about traders is that they fail. They lose money, and a large percentage of those traders are not gaining the education that you are receiving from reading this book. They're going to be using live trading strategies that are not even hammered out, they will just be haphazardly trading a little of this and a little of that until their account is gone, and then they will wonder what happened. You don't want to live trade a new strategy until you've proven that it's worth investing in. You may practice three months in a simulator, and then trade small size with real money for one month, and then go back to the simulator to work on your mistakes or practice new strategies for another three months. There is no shame in going back to a simulator at any stage of your day trading career. Even experienced and professional traders, when they want to develop a new strategy, test it out in a live simulator first.

Your focus while reading this book and practicing in simulated accounts should be to develop a strategy worth trading, and it's my pleasure to assist you with that process. Remember, the market is always going to be there. You don't need to rush this. A day trading career is a marathon and not a sprint. It's not about making $50,000 by the end of next week. It's about developing a set of skills that will last a lifetime.

Trading Based on the Time of Day

I categorize day trading sessions based upon the time of day: the Open, Mid-day, and the Close. Each time period should be treated differently, and you have to be careful because not all strategies are effective in every time period. Good traders make note of what time of day their most profitable trades occur and adjust their trading and strategies to fit such times.

The Open tends to last about 1.5 hours (9:30 to 11 a.m. New York time). I trade with the most size, and most frequency, during the Open, which statistically is my most profitable time period. As such, I increase my size during this time and make more trades.

- Bull Flag Momentum and VWAP trades tend to be the best strategies for the Open.

During the Mid-day (11 a.m. to 3 p.m.) the market is slower. This is the most dangerous time of the day. There is less volume and liquidity. A small order can cause a stock to move much more than you would anticipate. Strange and unexpected moves will stop you out more frequently during the Mid-day. A review of my trades indicates that I do the worst during the Mid-day. Accordingly, should I decide to trade during the Mid-day, I lower my share size and keep my stops tight. I will only make trades that offer the best risk/reward during this period. New traders tend to overtrade at Mid-day. At times, good trading, and smart trading, is to not be trading at all. It is best to gather information during the Mid-day in preparation for the Close. Watch the stocks, prepare for the Close, and be very, very careful with any trading you do.

- Reversal, VWAP, Moving Average, and Support or Resistance trades tend to be the best strategies for the Mid-day. I never trade Bull Flag Momentum in Mid-day or at the Close.

Into the Close (3 to 4 p.m.), stocks are more directional, so I stick with those that are trending up or down in the last hour of the trading day. I raise my tier size from the Mid-day, but not as high as it is at the Open. The daily closing prices tend to reflect the opinion of Wall Street traders on the value of stocks. They watch the markets throughout the day and tend to dominate the last hour of trading. Many of the market professionals take profits at that time to avoid carrying trades overnight. If the stock is moving higher in the last hour, it means the professionals are probably bullish on that stock. If the stock is moving lower in the last hour, the market professionals are probably bearish. It is thus a good idea to trade with the professionals and not against them.

- VWAP, Support or Resistance, and Moving Average trades tend to be the best strategies for the Close.

Many traders lose during the day what they have profited in the Open. Don't be one of them. I created a rule for myself. I am not allowed to lose more than 30% of what I have made in the Open during Mid-day and the Close. If I lose more than the allowed 30%, then I either stop trading or start trading in a simulator.

Chapter 8:
Step-by-Step to a Successful Trade

Now let's take a look at one of my trades. Later I'll explain in detail how I did it.

Building a Watchlist

On the morning of June 2, 2016, before the market Open, SRPT hit my watchlist scanner. Please see Figure 8.1 below. It was gapping down 14.5%, had a relatively low float (only 36 million shares, which meant the stock had the potential for good movement intraday) and a high Average True Range of $1.86 (which meant the stock on average moves in a range as large as $1.86 during the day). Higher ATRs are desirable for day trading.

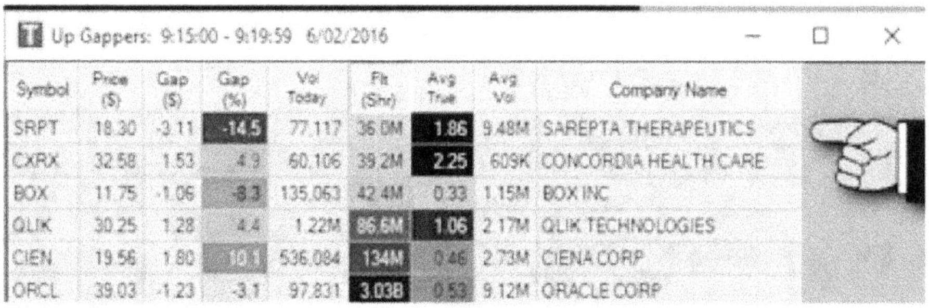
Up Gappers: 9:15:00 - 9:19:59 6/02/2016

Symbol	Price ($)	Gap ($)	Gap (%)	Vol Today	Flt (Shr)	Avg True	Avg Vol	Company Name
SRPT	18.30	-3.11	-14.5	77,117	36.0M	1.86	9.48M	SAREPTA THERAPEUTICS
CXRX	32.58	1.53	4.9	60,106	39.2M	2.25	609K	CONCORDIA HEALTH CARE
BOX	11.75	-1.06	-8.3	135,063	42.4M	0.33	1.15M	BOX INC
QLIK	30.25	1.28	4.4	1.22M	86.6M	1.06	2.17M	QLIK TECHNOLOGIES
CIEN	19.56	1.80	10.1	536,084	134M	0.46	2.73M	CIENA CORP
ORCL	39.03	-1.23	-3.1	97,831	3.03B	0.53	9.12M	ORACLE CORP

Figure 8.1 - My watchlist at 6:15 a.m. (9:15 a.m. New York time) - SRPT is on my watchlist.

Trading Plan (entry, exit, and stop loss)

I looked at the chart and decided to wait and see the price action for the first ten minutes of trading. You can follow along with my commentary in Figure 8.2. When the market opened, I saw that the buyers could not push the price any higher. There was no interest in buying back the stock. Therefore, I decided to do a VWAP trade. I monitored VWAP and the price action around VWAP for two 5-minute candlesticks. I realized that the sellers were in control and that the buyers could not push the price higher than VWAP and hold it. I knew it must be a good short with a stop above VWAP.

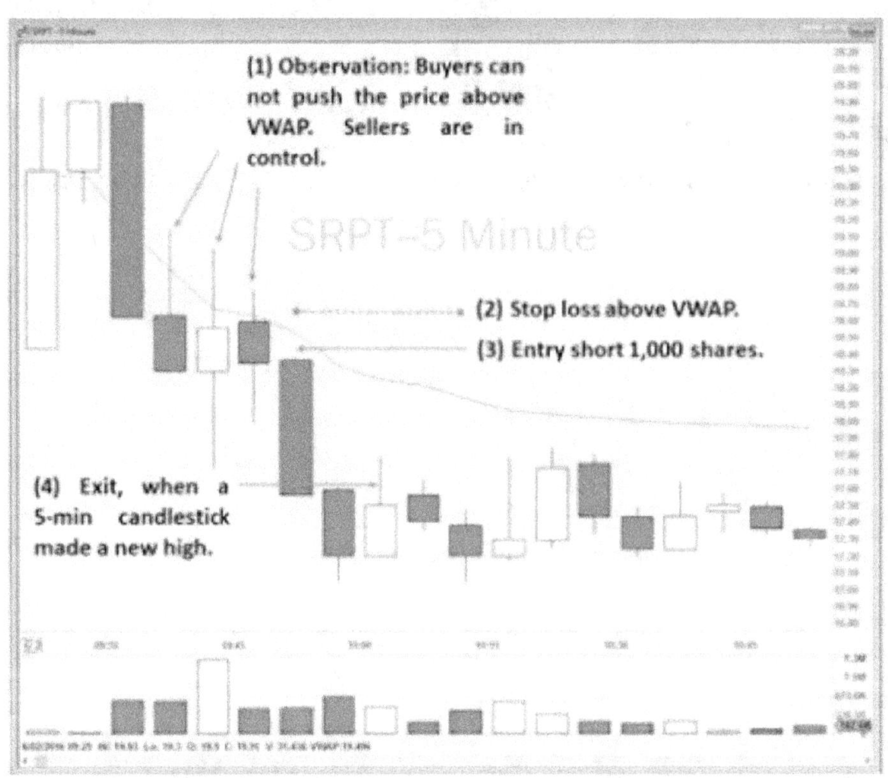

Figure 8.2 - 5-minute chart on June 2, 2016. Market opened at 9:30 a.m. New York time.

Execution

After ten minutes, when SRPT closed below VWAP, I entered the trade by shorting stock around $18.20 with a stop loss in mind just above VWAP. As expected, the sellers took control, and the stock price tanked to $17. I exited when a new 5-minute chart made a new high. When the candlestick made a new high, it meant that the buyers were then gaining control. I covered my shorts at around $17.40 and locked in a $650 profit, as you can see in Figure 8.3 below.

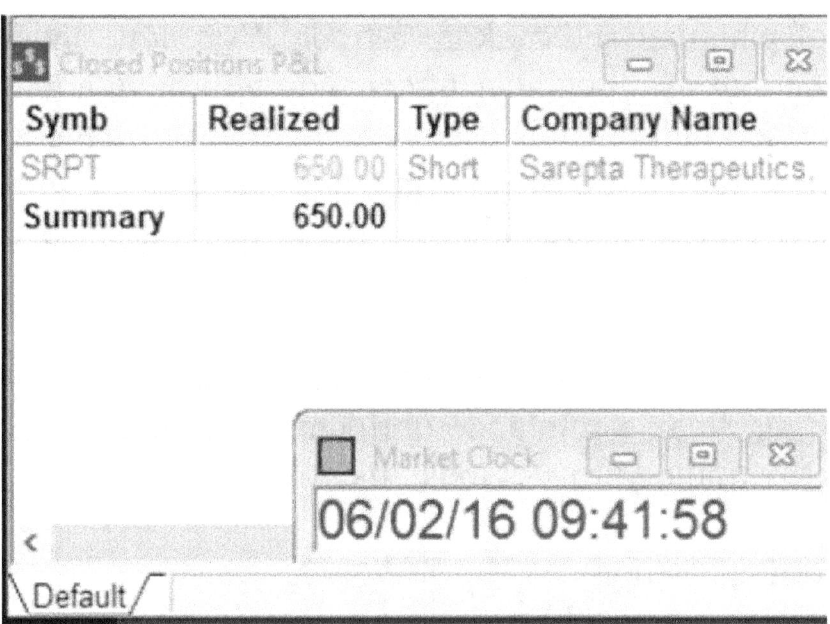

Figure 8.3 - My profit on June 2, 2016 (only 12 minutes into my day).

How Did I Do It?

My philosophy in trading is that you need to master only a few solid setups to be consistently profitable. In fact, having a simple trading method consisting of a few minimal setups will help to reduce confusion and stress and allow you to concentrate more on the psychological aspect of trading, which is truly what separates the winners from the losers.

Now that you have learned the basics of a few trading strategies, let's review the actual process of planning and making a trade. You now understand the setup you want to trade, but as a beginner trader, you will have a hard time planning and initiating a trade beforehand. It is very common to have a good setup but then enter or exit a trade at the wrong time and lose money while everyone else is making money. I believe the solution lies in developing a process for your trading. Plan a trade, and trade a plan.

I have a Ph.D. in chemical engineering, so I firmly believe in the process approach to trading. I can safely and confidently say that this is a major reason for my success. My trading process looks like this:

- Morning routine
- Develop my watchlist
- Organize a trade plan
- Initiate the trade according to plan
- Execute the trade according to plan
- Journaling and reflection

You must remember that what makes a trade profitable is the correct execution of all of the steps in the above process. Write down your reasons for entering and exiting every trade. Everyone can read this book or dozens of other books, but only a few people have the discipline to execute correctly. You might have a good setup but select a wrong stock to trade, such as a stock that is being manipulated by computers and institutional traders. Perhaps you will find a proper stock to trade, but you will enter the trade at the wrong time. A bad entry will make a mess of your plan and you will eventually lose your money. You can find a good stock to trade and enter a trade correctly, but if you don't exit properly, you will turn a winning trade into a losing one. All of the steps of the process are important.

Think about something significant that you do frequently in your life, and then think of how it can best be done. Now, consider how you do it currently. This is a great thought process for traders to have. When you take a trade, you need to ensure that you are focused on the right things both prior to entering it as well as during the trade. Creating a system for this thought process will take away most of the emotional hang-ups traders experience when looking to enter into a trade as well as managing it while they are in it.

This brings you to my final rule:

Rule 11: Profitable trading does not involve emotion. If you are an emotional trader, you will lose your money.

Education and practice give you a perspective of what matters in trading, how you trade, and how you can grow and develop your skills. Once you have a perspective on what matters, you can proceed to identify the specific processes on which to focus. The key to success is knowing your exact processes. Often you will learn them the hard way - by losing money.

I have found that trading, sticking to my plan and the discipline inherent in my trading methodology have had a snowball effect of positive habits in my life in general, and these habits have contributed to even more trading success. For example, I start my trading process by following the same routine when I get up each morning. I always go for a morning run before the trading session starts. As I mentioned before, I live in Vancouver, Canada, and the market opens at 6:30 a.m. my time. I wake up at 5 a.m. every morning. I go for a run from 5 to 5:45 a.m. (usually between 7 and 10 kilometers (4 to 6 miles)). I come home, take a shower, and at 6 a.m. start developing my plan.

I have found that when my body has not been active prior to trading, I will make poor decisions. There are scientific studies showing that aerobic exercise has a positive effect on the decision making process. People who regularly participate in an aerobic exercise (such as running for at least thirty minutes) have higher scores on neuropsychological functioning and performance tests that measure such cognitive functions as attentional control, inhibitory control, cognitive flexibility, working memory updating and capacity, and information processing speed. You can easily read about these topics on the Internet. Very often, our moods are influenced by our physical state, even by factors as delicate as what and how much we eat. Keep a record of your daily trading results as a function of your physical condition and you will see these relationships for yourself. Begin preventive maintenance by keeping body, and thus mind, in their peak operating condition. I stopped drinking coffee and alcohol, and I have stopped eating animal-based food, and my performance levels have increased significantly. Not eating meat and fish (any living beings that are marked with blood), and not using alcohol, coffee, tobacco and all other drugs lifts you above the curse and accelerates you forward in every facet of life. Likewise, in trading, your focus should be about being better than your current state, in all aspects of your life.

In day trading, simply being better than average is not sufficient. You must be significantly above the crowd to win in day trading. Unfortunately, day trading often appeals to impulsive people, gamblers, and those who feel that the world owes them a living. You cannot be one of them, and you should not act like one of them. You need to start developing the discipline of a winner. Winners think, feel, and act di f f erently than losers. You must look within yourself, discard your illusions, and change your old ways of being, thinking and acting. Change is hard, but if you want to be a successful trader, you must work on changing and developing your personality. To succeed, you will need motivation, knowledge, and discipline.

In 2014, I was visiting New York City and decided to go for a walk along Wall Street during lunchtime on a working day and perhaps take a selfie with Charging Bull, the famous 3.5-ton bronze sculpture of a bull located near Wall Street that symbolizes New York's financial industry.

I assumed that most of the people walking around in that area in a weekday must either be traders or working in the financial sector. I knew there was a good chance that the person sitting next to me in a coffee shop was taking home a 2-million-dollar bonus at the end of the year. I tried to observe people's attitudes, how they walked, how they dressed and how they treated themselves. I rarely saw anyone who was not well-dressed, without confidence and without being in excellent physical shape. I wondered to myself, are these people well-dressed, confident, in great physical shape and disciplined because they are rich and successful or did they become rich and successful because they were disciplined, confident and ambitious? I think this is a chicken and egg problem with no real answer, but I believe it is the latter. Based on what I saw, successful traders have often succeeded in almost everything they have done. They are ambitious and they expect a lot from themselves and they expect it at an early age. They expect to be the best. Success has been their history, so why should trading be any different?

Winners think, feel, and act di f f erently than losers. If you want to know if you have the self-discipline of a winner, try right now, starting today, to stop a habit that has challenged you in the past. If you have always wanted to be in better physical shape, try adding exercises such as running into your routine, and also take control of your salt and sugar intake. If you drink too much alcohol or coffee, try to see if for one month you can stay away from them. These are excellent tests to see if you are emotionally and intellectually strong enough or not to discipline yourself in the face of a losing trade. I am not saying that if you drink coffee or alcohol, or that if you are not a regular runner, you cannot become a successful trader, but if you make a try at these types of improvements and fail, then you should know that exercising self-control in trading will not be any easier to accomplish. Change is hard, but if you wish to be a successful trader, you need to work on changing and developing your personality at every level.

Often traders who fail to make money in trading get frustrated and go out and study more about the market to learn new strategies and additional technical indicators. They don't realize that their lack of self-discipline, impulsive behavior and their bad life habits are the main cause of their failure, not their technical knowledge.

As discussed previously, trading cannot be looked at as a hobby. You must approach trading seriously. As such, I wake up at 5 a.m., go for a 30-to-45 minute run, take a shower, get dressed, and eat oatmeal for breakfast prior to firing up my trading station at 6 a.m. I am awake, alert, and motivated when I sit down and start building my watchlist. This morning routine has tremendously helped my mental preparation for coming into the market. So, whatever you do, starting the morning out in a similar fashion will pay invaluable dividends. Rolling out of bed and throwing water on your face fifteen minutes in advance just does not give you sufficient time to be prepared for the market's opening. Sitting at your computer in your pajamas or underwear does not put you in the right mindset to attack the market. I know, because I have experienced all of these scenarios.

My watchlist comes from a specific scan that I use every morning. I will not look anywhere else because I am confident that the stocks on that scanner will have the best opportunity to set up for me to trade. I will vet each stock in the same way, using a checklist to determine if it is actually tradeable for me. My watchlist is built by 6:15 a.m., and I will not add anything to it after that time because there won't be enough time to review new stocks and plan for a trade. This allows me to watch the tickers on my watchlist for the fifteen minutes prior to opening. This actually leads into the next step in my process.

During the fifteen minutes prior to opening, I watch the tickers on my watchlist and develop trade plans for them based on the price action I am seeing. This is the most difficult part, and it requires experience, knowledge and education. Many traders fail at this step. When the bell rings at 6:30 a.m. (9:30 a.m. New York time), I'll have my plans in place, written on note cards because it is too easy to forget what I've seen on each ticker coming into the Open. What is my plan if it sets up to the long side? What's my plan if it sets up to the short side? What setup do I want to see? What are my profit targets? Where will my stop be? Is the profit window large enough for the trade to make sense? Just asking yourself questions like these when you are planning your trades will give you a significant advantage because you can then go in with a battle plan and stick to it. If it is written down close to my face I can easily refer to it, and that eliminates the anxiety that I used to feel when the opening bell rang. All I am doing at the opening is looking for my signal and trigger to enter the trade.

In the above example, I saw that SRPT had gapped down 14.5% (please see Figure 8.1). I knew that there wasn't much interest in buying the stock. Who would dare to buy when a stock gapped down almost 15% overnight? Most investors will be actually trying to get out and sell before the stock goes down even further, as though there's something seriously wrong with the company. I could not find any support or resistance nearby, therefore I decided to watch VWAP and I chose a VWAP short trade, as outlined in Figure 8.2.

Once the stock sets up, signals, and triggers an entry, I will enter without question (well, that's the plan anyway). Sometimes I may second-guess myself, but not too often. I have my profit targets written out on my trade plan, as well as the technical level that I am basing my stops on, so after entry I am just concentrating on hitting my marks and booking profit. There are some that say that knowing when to exit is the hardest part of the trade. It can be extremely tough not to exit the trade too early if you do not have a pre-set plan. If you have a plan ahead of time and you stick to it, you will have a much better chance of letting your winning trades work and cutting your losses off quickly instead of the other way around. This will also help with managing your emotions while in the trade. Recently I talked to one of my students about filtering out the noise. This strategy goes a long way to help do that so you can focus on the trade.

Once the trade is done, I will reflect on how well my plan worked and how well I stuck to what I had written. Most of the reflection on my trades will come in the evening when I review and recap my trades from the day. I believe one of the key things forgotten by many is reflection. "What did I do right?", "What did I do wrong?" and "Should I have sold earlier?" are all extremely important questions for the development of your trading strategies. Just because you made a good profit does not mean you are a perfect trader. How you play both sides of the table is extremely important. Write down or do a video recap of the trade and everything that comes to mind lesson-wise, and then file it away with other past lessons, and use them all as a reference for the future. Some lessons hit harder than others, but be confident that with time you will only get better. It only takes one incident of getting your hand slammed in a door to figure out that you must be more careful, but it may take two or three times to learn to turn on the lights before walking around your house at night.

Why is this process in trading important? This process is important because it describes how things are done to prepare for a trade and then provides the focus for executing them. It helps to filter out the emotional social noise and gives you a better chance for a more successful winning trade. It provides you with a tool to go back to and reflect on your trades and makes you a better trader. If you focus on the right processes, in the right way, you can design your way to trading success.

Chapter 9:
Next Steps for Beginner Traders

Successful day trading is based on three important skills.

1. You need to constantly analyze the balance of power between buyers and sellers and bet on the winning group (Chapter 6).
2. You need to practice excellent money and trade management (Chapter 3).
3. And you need sufficient self-discipline to follow your trading plan, to avoid getting overexcited or depressed in the markets, and to resist the temptation to make emotional decisions.

The Seven Fundamentals for Day Trading

To become a consistently profitable trader you need to follow these seven fundamental steps before entering into the world of trading. Some of them you should do before and after each and every single trade you make:

1. Education and simulated trading
2. Preparation
3. Hard work
4. Patience
5. Discipline
6. Mentorship and a community of traders
7. Reflection and review

Education and Simulated Trading

Now that you have read this book, you should be in a better position to make a decision on whether or not day trading is right for you. Day trading requires a certain mindset, as well as a discipline and a set of skills that not everyone possesses. Interestingly, most of the traders I know are also poker players. They enjoy speculation and the stimulation that comes from it. Although poker is a type of gambling, day trading is not. Day trading is a science, a skill, and a career, and has nothing to do with gambling. It is the serious business of selling and buying stocks, at times in a matter of seconds. You should be able to make decisions fast, with no emotion or hesitation. Doing otherwise results in losing real money.

After you've made up your mind and decided that you want to start day trading, the next step is to get a proper education. This book equips you with the basic knowledge essential for day trading, but you still have a long way to go before you will be a consistently profitable trader. Can you be a mechanic by just reading a book? Can you perform surgery after reading a book or taking First Aid 101? No. This book develops a foundation that you can build upon. This book introduces straightforward trading setups to simply show what day trading looks like. It is not meant by any means to be a stand-alone book. You are not a trader yet, not even close.

I encourage you to read more books and find online or in-person courses on day trading. New traders often search for the best traders on the Internet. They think that learning from the most experienced traders is the best way to learn. On the contrary, I think new traders should look for the best "teacher". There is a difference. Sometimes the best trader has no personality, or poor people skills, while a consistently profitable, but not one of the top 10 traders, can emerge as a premier lecturer, communicator, and mentor. New traders need to find the best teacher. You don't need to learn from the best traders to become the best trader. Think about who some of the best professional sports coaches are. Often they were not superstar players. They knew the sport, but their passion was for teaching and developing players. The skills needed to become a great trader are different from those required to be an effective trading coach. Being a star trader requires superior pattern recognition and discipline. On the other hand, effective trading coaches are often obsessed with finding better ways to teach, are patient, and communicate clearly and effectively in a simple and easy-to-understand language. They can explain their methodology coherently. Often great traders lack the monetary incentive to create the best training program.

Trading in a Simulator

You should never start your day trading career with real money. Sign up with one of the brokers that provides you with simulated accounts with real market data. Some brokers give you access to delayed market data, but don't use those. You need to make decisions real time. Most of the simulated data software is a paid service, so you need to save some money for that software. Many trading rooms and trading educators offer simulator accounts. DAS Trader offers the best simulated accounts for $120 per month (at the time of writing). Check out their website (www.dastrader.com) or contact them at support@dastrader.com for more information. This completes my unpaid and unsolicited advertisement for them!

If you use it for six months, and trade only with simulated money, it will cost you just $720. This is the cost of a proper education. If you are seriously considering day trading as a career, it's a small expenditure compared to the cost of an education for a new profession. For example, imagine that you want to go to school to get an MBA - it will easily cost you over $50,000. Likewise, many other diploma or post-graduation programs cost significantly more than the education required for day trading.

Once you have a simulated account, you will need to develop your strategy. Try the strategies that I have discussed in this book, and master one or two of them that fit with your personality, available time, and trading platform. There is no best strategy among them, just like there is no best automobile in the market. There might, however, be a best car for you. The VWAP, Support or Resistance, and the Opening Range Breakout Strategies are the easiest and my favorites. You need to only master a few of them to always be profitable in the market. Keep your strategy simple. When you have a solid strategy that you've mastered, make sure there is no emotion attached to it. Keep practicing it, and then start practicing a second strategy, and learn to incrementally add size in those strategies.

Practice with the amounts of money that you will be trading in real life. It is easy to buy a position worth $100,000 in a simulated account and watch it lose half of its value in a matter of seconds. But could you tolerate this loss in a real account? No. You will probably become an emotional trader and make a decision quickly, usually resulting in a major loss. Always trade in the simulator with the size and position that you will be using in the real account. Otherwise, there is no point in trading in a simulated account. Move to a real account only after at least three months of training with a simulated account and then, start small, with real money. Trade small while you're learning or when you are feeling stressed. If you wish, you can always have a chat with me in our chatroom and receive some advice and guidance.

New traders often try to skip steps in the process, lose their money, and then give up their day trading career forever and tell themselves that it is impossible to make money by day trading. Remember, baby steps. Success in day trading is one foot forward and then the next. Master one topic, and then and only then move on to the next.

Most traders struggle when they first begin, and many do not have sufficient time in the morning to practice in real time. Those who can give trading more time when they start have a better chance to succeed. How long does it take to be a consistently profitable trader? I don't think anyone can become a consistently profitable trader in less than three or four months. After four months of paper trading, you need at least another three months of trading in small share size to master your emotions and practice self-discipline and defensive money management while trading with real money. After six months, you may become a seasoned trader. Eight months is probably better than six months, and twelve months is perhaps better than both. Are you patient enough for this learning curve? Do you really want this career? Then you should be patient enough. Do you have this much time to learn the day trading profession?

It always amuses me when I see books or online courses and websites that offer trading education that will make a person money starting on day one! I wonder who would believe such advertisements.

You must define a sensible process oriented goal for yourself, such as: *I want to learn how to day trade. I do not want to make a living out of it for now.* Do not set an absolute income for yourself in day trading, not at least for the first two years. This is very important. Many traders think of inspiring goals such as making a million dollars or being able to trade for a living from a beach house in the Caribbean. These goals may be motivating, and they definitely have their place, but they distract you from focusing on what you need to do today and tomorrow to become better. What you as a new trader can control is the process of trading: how to make and execute sound trading decisions. Your daily goal should be to trade well, not to make money. The normal uncertainty of the market will result in some days or weeks being in the red.

Often new traders email and ask me how they can become full-time traders while they are working at a different job from 9 a.m. to 5 p.m. New York time. I really don't have any answer for that. They probably cannot become a full-time trader if they cannot trade in a simulator real time between 9:30 and 11:30 a.m. New York time. You do not need to have the whole day available for trading, but you at least need the first two hours of market Open. If you insist, I would say the first one hour of the market Open (9:30 to 10:30 a.m. New York time) is the absolute minimum time you should be available for trading and practice, in addition to any time you need for preparation before the market opens at 9:30 a.m. New York time. Sometimes I am done with trading and hit my daily goal by 9:45 a.m., but sometimes I need to watch the market longer to find trading opportunities. Do you have this flexibility in your work-life schedule?

When I started day trading, I was unemployed. Then I had to find a job to pay the bills because I was losing my savings on day trading. I am lucky I live in Vancouver (in the Pacific time zone) because I could trade and practice between 6:30 and 8:30 a.m. and then be at work for 9 a.m. Pacific time. If you don't have this luxury, maybe swing trading is better for you. But making a living out of swing trading is more difficult. The best swing traders can expect an annual return of 20% on their account size. Day traders, on the other hand, look to profit between 0.5-1% of their account size daily. The currency market (Forex) is open 24 hours/5 days per week, and perhaps you could consider trading currencies and commodities if you do not have sufficient free time to practice day trading or swing trading. This book though is not a useful guide for swing trading or for the Forex market. They are both different from day trading in so many ways.

You must always be continuing your education and reflecting upon your trading strategy. Never stop learning about the stock market. The market is a dynamic environment and it's constantly changing. Day trading is different than it was ten years ago, and it will be different in another ten years. So keep reading and discussing your progress and performance with your mentors and other traders. Always think ahead and maintain a progressive and winning attitude.

Learn as much as you can, but keep a degree of healthy skepticism about everything, including this book. Ask questions, and do not accept experts at their word. Consistently profitable traders constantly evaluate their trading system. They make adjustments every month, every day, and even intraday. Every day is new. It is about developing trading skills, discipline, and controlling emotions, and then making adjustments continually. That is *How to Day Trade for a Living*.

Consistently profitable traders try to learn the process of trading and make good and fundamentally correct trades without thinking about the money. This is, of course, the opposite of amateurs, who are obsessed with making money every single day. Such thinking is your worst enemy. I am not trying to make money as a trader. My focus is on "doing the right thing". All I am looking for is excellent risk/reward opportunities. And then I trade them. Being good at trading requires mastering the process of trading and the fundamentals of a good trade. Money is just the by-product of executing fundamentally solid trades.

As a new trader, you will be constantly looking at your profit and loss (P&L). P&L is the most emotionally distracting column in my trading platform. Plus $250, negative $475, plus $1,100. I tend to make irrational decisions by looking at it. I used to panic and sell my position when my P&L became negative although my trade was still valid according to my plan. Or, quite often, I became greedy and sold my winning position too early while my profit target had yet to be reached according to my plan. I did myself a favor and I hid my P&L column. I trade based on technical levels and the plan I make. I don't look at how much I am up or down in real time.

I'll note again, your P&L is not important when you first begin trading with real money, especially when you trade in smaller share sizes. On most trading platforms, there is an option to hide your real time P&L. If yours doesn't have it, then go old school and use some dark masking tape. I say this seriously. I encourage you to go and find some masking tape and slap it on your screen. Your goal is to develop trading skills and not to make money. You have to focus on getting better every single day, one trade after another. That is *How to Day Trade for a Living*. Push your comfort zone to find greater success.

Preparation

John Wooden (or as some call him, the Wizard of Westwood), the famous American basketball player and coach, once said, "By failing to prepare, you are preparing to fail." Indeed.

There are two aspects to the preparation process for day traders:

1) the preparation necessary before the market opens (usually the night before or between 8 and 9:30 a.m. New York time), and

2) the specific trading information you must obtain before you can make a trade.

Wake up on time and get behind your PC early.

Review your scanners and shortlist your choices of stocks for the day. Review www.finviz.com or www.briefing.com and read about the fundamental catalysts that caused the stock to gap up or down. Compile information such as daily volume, intraday range, and short interest. Review daily charts and identify important levels of support or resistance. I do not make a trade unless I know the average volume, Average True Range, important technical levels, short interest, and fresh news for the Stocks in Play.

Shortlist your watchlist down to two or three stocks. During earnings season, there are many Stocks in Play to choose from. Each day, traders shouldn't choose more than two or three of these stocks to focus on. You can make considerably more money trading one or two stocks well instead of watching and trading many stocks poorly.

The earlier you start your morning the more time you will have to go through the news and find the best Stocks in Play. Sometimes in those extra minutes you find the stock of the day that you wouldn't have if you had spent less time researching. Moreover, you have extra time to ask members of your community about their choices of stocks and obtain their feedback. Most professional traders do not arrive later than 7:30 a.m. New York time. Certainly experienced traders with a strong community and powerful scanners can stroll in later, but 9 a.m. is the latest that most serious traders arrive. Prepare physically. Drink enough water to hydrate during the morning stretch and do not become over caffeinated.

Being present in the pre-market is important. Every once in a while there will be an opportunity during pre-market trading to make quick money on a breaking news story. In addition, valuable information can be obtained by watching how stocks are being traded in the pre-market. Monitor the ranges of the stocks that are on your watchlist, identify intraday support or resistance levels, and confirm how much volume is being traded.

Often new traders will think that trading strategies can be reduced to a few rules that they must follow to be profitable: *always do this or always do that*. Wrong. Trading isn't about "always" at all; it is about each single trade, and each situation. Every trade is a new puzzle that you must solve. There is no universal answer to all of the puzzles in the market. Therefore, you need to make a plan for each trade as early as when you are doing your pre-market scanning. Before making a trade, you must create a plan for your trades or a series of *"if-then"* statements. Develop some plans as to when you might take a position in one of your stocks on your watchlist. If you see the *x* scenario, then you will buy at this price. Continue creating "if-then" scenarios for each outcome.

For an example, let's take a look at Figures 9.1 and 9.2. Imagine you plan to trade DICK'S Sporting Goods, Inc. (ticker: DKS) on March 7, 2017. The stock had gapped down because of disappointing earnings reports and was being traded at around $50.50 at the pre-market. You think it might be a Stock in Play.

Symbol								Sector
MOMO	28.96	1,208,247	2.35	8.8	113.45M	1.07		Management of Companies and Enterprise
DISH	64.25	386.878	3.02	4.9	201.27M	1.08	7.80	Information
FRC	95.65	102.409	-1.31	-1.4	153.09M	1.44		Finance and Insurance
DKS	50.45	455.668	-2.16	-4.1	87.89M	1.63	7.73	Retail Trade
SNAP	22.53	1,625.320	-1.24	-5.2	775.61M	4.72		Information

Figure 9.1 - My watchlist at 6 a.m. (9 a.m. New York time) on March 7, 2017 - DKS is on my watchlist.

Consider the different ways the stocks you have picked might trade and develop a series of **if-then** scenarios such as I've marked on Figure 9.2 below:

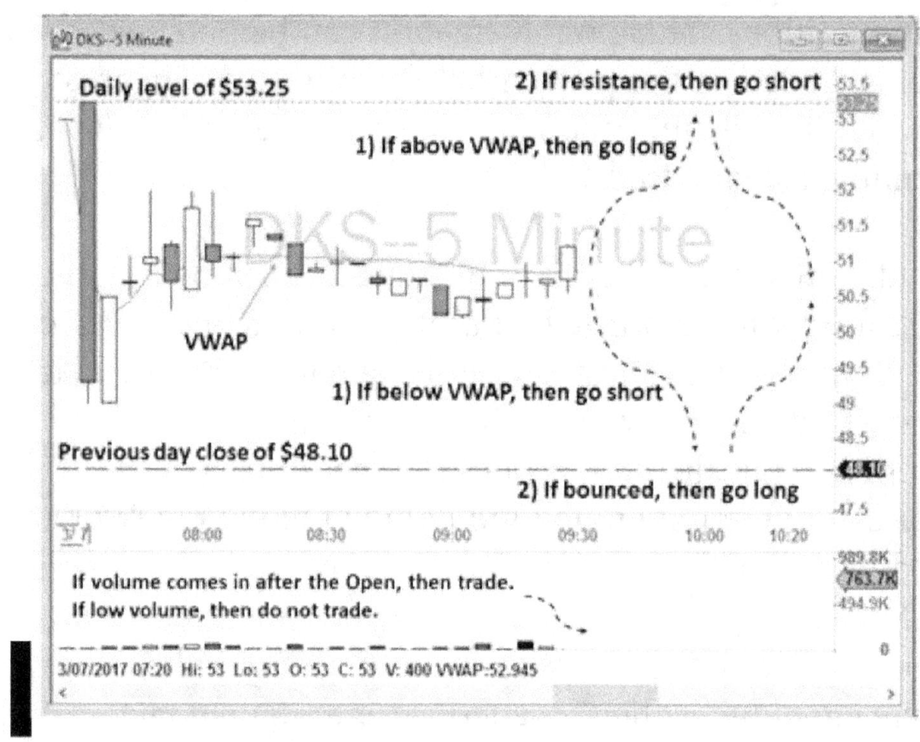

Figure 9.2 - Pre-market 5-minute chart of DKS on March 7, 2017 with my if-then statements noted. Market will open at 9:30 a.m. New York time.

If the price cannot push higher than VWAP in the first fifteen minutes of the market Open, **then** I will go short until the previous day close of $48.10.

If the price does sell off to the previous day close of $48.10, **then** I will go long and ride the reversal to the VWAP.

If the price pushes over VWAP with high volume, **then** I will go long and ride the momentum to sell at the next resistance level of $53.25.

If the price breaks over the daily level of $53.25, **then** I will go long again until the daily level of $55.50 (which is not shown on the above Figure 9.2).

On the other hand, **if** the price goes to $53.25, and that level acts as a strong resistance, **then** I will go short with the stock until it goes back down to VWAP.

You can write down your statements at the beginning of your trading career to make sure you stick to them, but after a few months of simulated trading you will learn how to quickly develop and review these statements in your mind. That is one of the most important outcomes of trading in a simulator: to practice and master if-then scenarios for your strategies and to process that information quickly. That is why three to six months of live simulated trading is essential as you begin your day trading career. As intraday traders, we develop theories daily.

In case you are wondering about DKS in the above example, it actually opened weak (below VWAP) and it was a good short trade toward the previous day close of $48.10 as you can see in Figure 9.3 below. I then caught a smaller bounce from the previous day close to the VWAP with a long position.

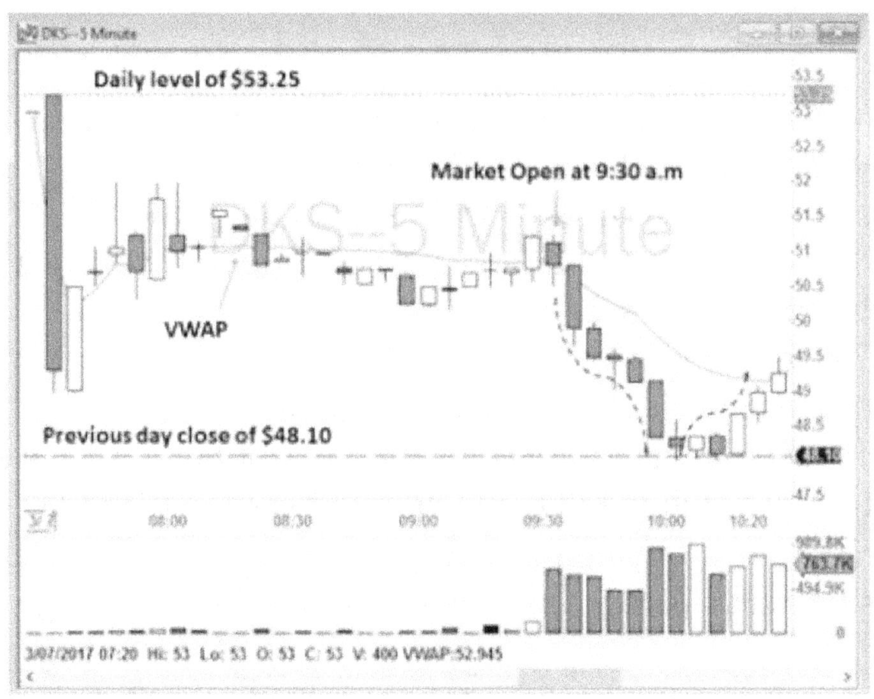

Figure 9.3 - 5-minute chart on March 7, 2017 and my profit for that day (I also traded MEET, MOMO and MYL but they are not shown here and are not relevant to this example).

Hard Work

Hard work in day trading is different from what you might originally assume. A trader should not work 120 hours a week like investment bankers or corporate lawyers or other highly paid professionals do because, for us day traders, there are no end of the year bonuses. More than anything else, day trading is perhaps most similar to being a professional athlete because it is judged by one's daily performance. Having said that, day traders should work hard, consistently and productively, each and every day. Watching your trading screens intently and gathering important market information is how we define hard work in day trading. You must ask the following questions constantly and at a rapid pace for several hours every day:

- Who is in control of the price: the buyers or the sellers?
- What technical levels are most important?
- Is this stock stronger or weaker than the market?
- Where is most of the volume being traded? At the VWAP? Or the first five minutes? Or near moving averages?
- How much volume at a price causes the stock to move up or down?
- What is the bid-ask spread? Is it tradeable?
- How quickly does the stock move? Is it being traded smoothly or is it choppy, jumping up and down with every trade?
- Is the stock trading in a particular pattern on a 5-minute chart? How is the stock being traded on a 1-minute chart?

These are some of the questions that I ask myself and then answer before trading a stock. All of this information should be gathered before you make any trade.

This is what we mean by hard work. As you can see, day trading is an intense intellectual pursuit which requires hard work. Remember Rule 2?

In addition, showing up every day to trade matters, either in your real account or in a simulator. If you search for support and resistance levels every day, including before the market opens, it will positively impact your trading in the long term. Turning off the PC early because a few trades went against you should be saved for special occasions when you really must clear your head. Professionals often mentally recover after a few bad losses by switching to a simulator. I always encourage new traders in the simulator to continue trading until the Close and to find good opportunities to practice, especially since traders in the simulator are not under the same emotional stress as traders trading their own real money are. Of course, that does not mean that new traders should practice overtrading. Even when practicing in a simulator, with no commission and no real P&L, you should only trade sound strategies with excellent risk/reward opportunities.

I am often asked: "When you were in your first months of trading, did you ever feel like you couldn't do it?" The answer is YES, many times. I still, at least once a month, get really frustrated after a few bad losses and consider quitting day trading. Many times in my trading career I have wanted to quit and at times I have actually believed the myth that day trading is impossible. But I did not quit. I really desired to be a successful trader. I wanted the lifestyle and the freedom that comes with it. I paid the price for my mistakes, I focused on my education, and I eventually survived the very difficult learning curve of trading.

Patience

To become a consistently profitable trader, not only must you prepare properly and work hard, but you must also have patience.

Most successful trades are easy when you look at them after the fact, but finding them in real time is difficult and requires patience and hard work.

Watch, watch, and watch some more. If you are watching a stock, and it is not offering excellent risk/reward opportunities, then move on. Look at other stocks on your watchlist, and watch them intently. Consistently profitable traders spend trading days searching and watching for excellent risk/reward opportunities.

Successful traders are patient. They understand that they will not and should not be in every move. You should wait for opportunities with which you feel comfortable and confident. Professional traders realize that it is not enough to buy a strong stock, or sell short a weak one. Entry price is extremely important. You have to open your positions at a price that offers the best risk/reward opportunity. Do not trade a strong stock that has moved away from a good risk/reward entry. That is called *chasing the stock.*

For example, if a stock is trading near a support and then breaks out downward, and you see a short selling opportunity but miss it, well, that is your first mistake. But if, out of frustration, you sell short that same stock well below that level, you have chased it. Now you have made a bigger mistake. Chasing stocks is a deadly unforgivable sin in day trading. Missing the opportunity will not lose you any money (just an opportunity cost), but chasing the stock will. Do not let one mistake cause you to lose money with another one.

Discipline

Success in trading comes with skill development and self-discipline. Trading principles are easy, and day trading strategies are very simple. I have a Ph.D. in chemical engineering and I have worked as a research scientist at a world class facility. I have published numerous scholarly publications in high impact and respected scientific journals on my nanotechnology and complicated molecular level research. Believe me, I had to study and understand extremely more difficult concepts, so I can assure you that day trading, in theory at least, is easy.

What makes day trading, or any type of trading for that matter, difficult is the discipline and self-control that you need. You have no chance to make money as a trader without discipline, no matter your style, the time you commit to trading, the country you live in, or the market you are trading in.

Beginner traders who fail to make money in the markets often get frustrated and go out and try to learn more about how the markets work, study new strategies, adopt additional technical indicators, follow new traders, and join other chatrooms. They don't realize that the main cause of their failure is often their lack of self-discipline, their impulsive decisions and their sloppy risk and money management, not their technical knowledge.

Year after year, professional institutional traders perform so much better than private retail traders do. While most private traders are university-educated and thoughtful book-reading individuals who are often business owners or professionals, the average institutional traders are loud 20 something-year-old cowboys who used to play rugby in college and haven't read a book for many years. Have you wondered why these guys outperform private traders year after year? It's not because they are younger or sharper or faster. They also don't win because of their training or platforms, since most of us retail traders have almost the same gear as they do. The answer is the strictly enforced discipline of trading firms.

Many successful institutional traders will quit their firm and go out on their own. They ask themselves, "Why should I share all of my profits with the firm, when I know how to trade and can keep all of the profit for myself?" Most of them lose money as private traders. They equip themselves with the same software and platforms, trade the same systems, and stay in touch with their contacts, but still fail. After a few months, most of them are back in a New York City recruiting office, looking for a trading job. How come those traders could make money for their firms but not for themselves?

The answer is self-discipline.

When institutional traders quit their firm, they leave behind their manager and all of the strictly enforced risk control rules. A trader who violates risk limits is fired immediately. Traders who leave institutions may know how to trade, but their discipline is often external, not internal. They quickly lose money without their managers because they have developed no self-discipline.

We private retail traders can break any rule and change our plan in the middle of a trade. We can average down to a losing position, we can constantly break the rules, and no one will notice. Managers in trading firms though are quick to get rid of impulsive people who break any trading rule for a second time. This creates a serious discipline for institutional traders. Strict external discipline saves institutional traders from heavy losses and deadly sins (such as the averaging down of a losing position), which quite often will destroy many private accounts.

Discipline means you execute your plan and honor your stop loss as you set it out, without altering it in the middle of a trade. Discipline is executing your detailed plan every single time. If your plan is to buy a stock at VWAP and your stop loss is if it fails to hold VWAP, then you must accept the loss immediately and get out of the trade if the stock fails to hold the VWAP.

Do not be stubborn about your decision if you are wrong. The market does not reward stubbornness. The market is not interested in how you wish stocks would trade. Traders must adapt to the market and do what the market demands. And that is the way day trading works and that is how it will always work.

There are going to be many days when you follow your plan, like in the above example, and then the stock will go back up and trade above VWAP after you were stopped out. In fact, there will be many times such as this in your trading career. But consider these two points: (1) Do not judge your trading strategy based upon one trade. Executing your plan, and being disciplined, will lead to long-term success. Many times your plan will be fine and solid but a hedge fund manager out of nowhere will decide to liquidate a position in a stock that you are trading, the price will drop suddenly and you will get stopped out. You did not do anything wrong, it is the nature of the market that is unpredictable. At times, the uncertainty of the market will leave you in the red. (2) A professional trader accepts the loss and gets out of the trade. You then re-evaluate and plan another if-then scenario. You can always get back into the stock. Commissions are cheap (for most of the brokers), and professionals often take several quick stabs at a trade before it will start running in their favor.

Trading teaches you a great deal about yourself, about your mental weaknesses and about your strengths. This alone ensures that trading is a valuable life experience.

Mentorship and a Community of Traders

Dr. Brett Steenbarger, the author of great books such as *The Psychology of Trading* and *The Daily Trading Coach*, once wrote:

"There is no question in my mind that, if I were to start trading full-time, knowing what I know now, I would either join a proprietary trading firm or would form my own "virtual trading group" by connecting online (and in real time) with a handful of like-minded traders."

You need to be part of a mastermind group that will add value to your trading career. To whom can you turn to ask trading questions? I encourage you to join a community of traders. Trading alone is very difficult and can be emotionally overwhelming. It is very helpful to join a community of traders so that you can ask them questions, talk to them, learn new methods and strategies, get some hints and alerts about the stock market, and also make your own contributions. If you join me, you will see that I often lose money. It can be comforting to see that losing money is not limited to you, and everyone, including experienced traders, has to take a loss. As I've said, it's all part of the process.

There are many chatrooms that you can join on the Internet. Some of them are free, but most of them charge a fee. In our chatroom, you can see my trading platform and stock screener in real time while I am trading and listen as I explain my strategy and thought process. You can watch and listen. Or you can take your own trades, but still be part of our community.

It is extremely important to remember however, that if you are in any community of traders, either our chatroom at www.BearBullTraders.com or the dozens of others out there, you should not follow the pack or the room moderator, but you should be an independent thinker. Generally, people change when they join crowds. They become more unquestioning and impulsive, nervously searching for a leader whose trades they can mirror. They react with the crowd instead of using their minds. Chatroom members may catch a few trends together, but they get killed when trends reverse. Never forget that successful traders are independent thinkers. Simply use your judgment to decide when to trade and when not to.

You need to find a trading mentor. A good mentor can positively impact your trading career in so many different ways. Today, because of algorithmic programs and market volatility, it's much harder for new traders to survive the learning curve. A good mentor can make a huge difference. A mentor demonstrates the professionalism required to be successful. A mentor can lead you to discover the talent inside of you. Sometimes you just need to be told that you can do it. In online trading communities, experienced traders mentor new traders at times for a fee, but often for free. I personally mentor a few traders at a time, and of course, I myself did and still have a trading mentor. It is important to note though that mentorship does not work unless you are receptive, listen, and then put in the work necessary to adapt successfully.

You should find a mentor whose trading style fits with your personality. For example, if momentum trading is your favorite style, you're wasting your time talking to me. Although I trade them from time to time, my style is really only for those who have an intraday swing day mentality. I mostly focus on VWAP and Support or Resistance trades.

Reflection and Review

By now, you may correctly think that trading psychology and self-discipline, a series of proven trading strategies, and excellent money and risk management are the essential elements of success in trading. But there is another element that ties all of your trading fundamentals together: record-keeping.

Keeping records of your trades will enable you to learn from your past success and failure experiences and make you a better trader. In fact, the most important and the most effective way to continuously improve as a trader is to keep a diary of your trades. There are many consistently profitable traders around the world, trading different markets with different methods, but they all have one thing in common: they keep excellent records of their trades. It is a very tedious and boring task; but it is also a very necessary task. Journal your trades daily. Make sure to include the following points in your trading journal:

1. Your physical well-being (lack of sleep, too much coffee, too much food the night before, etc.)
2. The time of the day you made the trade
3. The strategy you were anticipating
4. How you found the opportunity (from a scanner, a chatroom, etc.)
5. Quality of your entry (risk/reward)
6. Sizing/management of your trade (scaling in and out as planned)
7. Execution of exits (following profit targets or stop losses)

I personally take a screenshot from my screen (with a free software called *Screenshot Captor*) and journal my trades in my blog with that software. Please visit my blog to get some ideas on how to journal your trades. You do not have to follow my style, but you should find what works best for you because to be successful, you must journal your trades daily.

Mike Bellafiore, co-founder of SMB Capital (a proprietary trading firm in New York City), writes in his book *One Good Trade* that the professional traders at his firm video record all of their trades during the day. In their afternoon session they sit around their conference room tables, enjoy a lunch catered by the firm, review their trades and groupthink about better ways to take your money. Trading is a full contact sport and anything less than your complete focus is disrespectful to the game and will certainly knock you out of the game. Profitable traders constantly evaluate their trading system. They make adjustments every month, every day, and even intraday.

New traders often ask me how to improve after a series of losses and a period of struggling. I recommend to them that they review their journal and look more specifically at what precisely they are doing poorly at in their trading. I am doing poorly doesn't mean anything. You cannot improve if you don't have a proper record of your daily trades.

- Is it your stock selection?
- Is it your entry points?
- Is it your discipline or psychology?
- Is it your platform or clearing firm (broker)?
- What about other traders, is it a bad month for everyone or just for you?

If the new trader lives in Vancouver, Canada, I usually meet them in person and identify the areas that need to be improved. If I cannot meet them in person, we have a chat over Skype and evaluate their performance. One time a trader complained about her order execution speed. I remotely connected to her PC (using TeamViewer, a remote control/remote access software) and evaluated the CPU performance. I had to remove many unnecessary programs and apps from her PC, run a malware scanner and remove a variety of intrusive software, computer viruses, spyware, adware, scareware, and other malicious programs. I freed up a lot of the PC's memory and CPU capacity and her trading execution speed increased significantly. Your PC, just like your body and mind, needs to be kept clean, lean and fast, all of which have a direct effect on your trading platform and eventually your trading results.

I personally live video record all of my trades during the morning session (as I rarely make any trades Mid-day or at the Close). I believe traders, like athletes, should watch their trading videos. The best athletes and teams watch films of themselves to see what they're doing right and wrong, and how best to improve. I will review my tapes during Mid-day and make sure to note important observations on my entry, exit, price action, Level 2 signals and so on. I try to learn as much as possible from my trades. Sometimes I look for new algorithmic programs that I must be aware of. I search for areas that I could have added more size. This is one of my trading weaknesses. I also do a poor job of holding for a longer time the stocks that are going in my favor. I therefore consider trades that I could have held longer. I make sure to find spots where I was too aggressive and to find trades that did not offer a good risk/reward opportunity but that I still took the trade in. I review my position sizing and why and where I added more. That is *How to Day Trade for a Living*. There is no other way to get better. There are no excuses in trading. To get better and to help traders in my community, I have to do this.

Watching trading videos also shows me how easy trading is when there are no emotions attached to a trade. When I review my work, I am not invested in a trade in real time with real money. Trading live, the market seems fast and unpredictable. When you watch back your trading video, you see that the market is actually very slow. There are times when I see the pattern in a stock by watching my video and recognize how I traded the stock backward, and that is embarrassing for someone of my experience.

I later review my videos over the weekend to create educational series to use in teaching day trading. Over the weekend, after I celebrate the winning week on Friday night with my friends and family in Vancouver, I lock myself into my home office and cut tape after tape to develop and update my training programs.

Watching your videos is an exercise that can benefit all traders no matter their experience. New traders need to watch the markets trade. Watching your videos increases your trading experience and confidence and significantly shortens your learning curve. But I agree, it takes time and it is indeed boring.

My Daily Blog and YouTube Video Recaps

As mentioned earlier, I also write a blog post about my trades and document my thoughts for each and every trade on my website. This blog helps me to maintain a good record of all of my trades, and also helps my fellow traders and others to learn more by reading about my experiences. Your journal does not have to be long and complicated, and it can include mostly images. As I noted, I use a free software called Screenshot Captor to take a screenshot from my platform in real time right after I end a trade. I can see my entries and exits on the chart and I just add my thought process to the journal along with anything else I think I should note from that trading day. Below you can read my daily blog for February 6, 2017: ---------

" +$986 Trading GALE TSN COG HAS
February 6, 2017

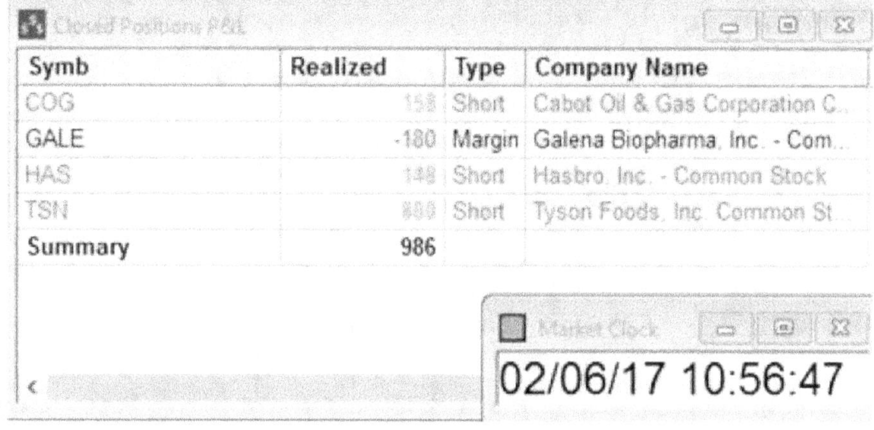

by Andrew

Figure 9.4 - My closed P&L on February 6, 2017.

Wow, what a day! Let's see:

GALE

GALE was very active pre-market, that is why I wanted to watch it. It opened weak below VWAP, but closed above it after the first 1 min. I went long 2,000 shares with the hope of getting to the pre-market high at $2.62.

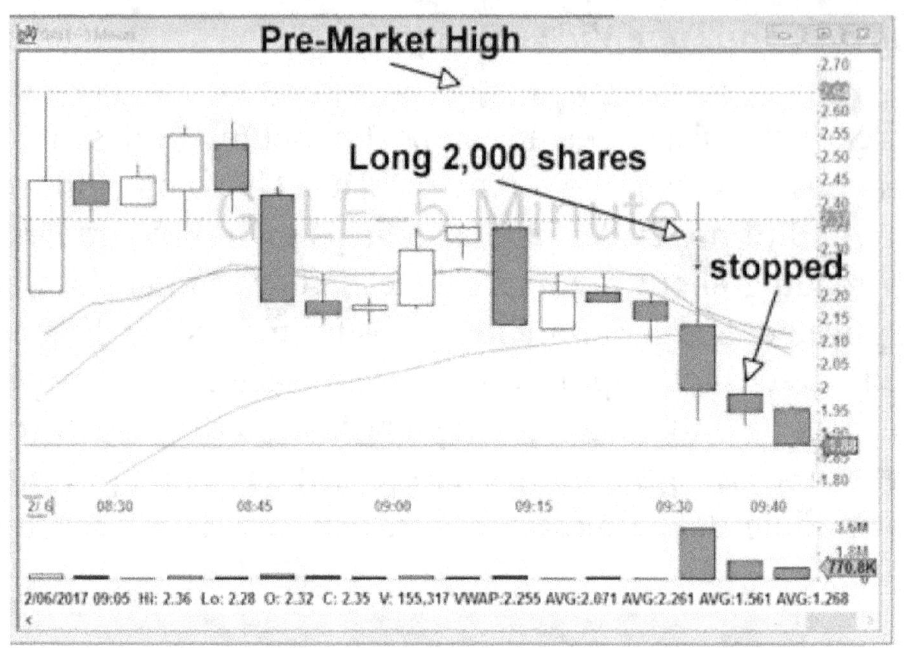

Figure 9.5 - 5-minute chart of GALE on February 6, 2017.

It could not push higher, and I got stopped out. Stock later sold off massively during the day, I am glad I got out of the way. -$180 loss.

Figure 9.6 - 1-minute chart of GALE on February 6, 2017.

TSN

TSN was a solid VWAP trade. I went short 400 shares below VWAP after the Opening Range Breakout. I covered in 4 steps toward the previous day close and *daily level of $64.47. I have never seen a stock sell off like this at the Open. Chop Chop!*

Stock bounced back to VWAP, rejected it, and sold off again. I went short 100 shares again below daily level of $64.47. I got stopped out early at VWAP. I should have waited to see if TSN broke the VWAP or not.

But price could not break the VWAP and sold off again. This time I went short small, and added 2 more times below VWAP with the profit target of daily level of $64.47. I covered everything at $64.47 daily level as planned. Chop Chop!

Damn I should have held some for next move down because we broke that level and stock is now moving lower.

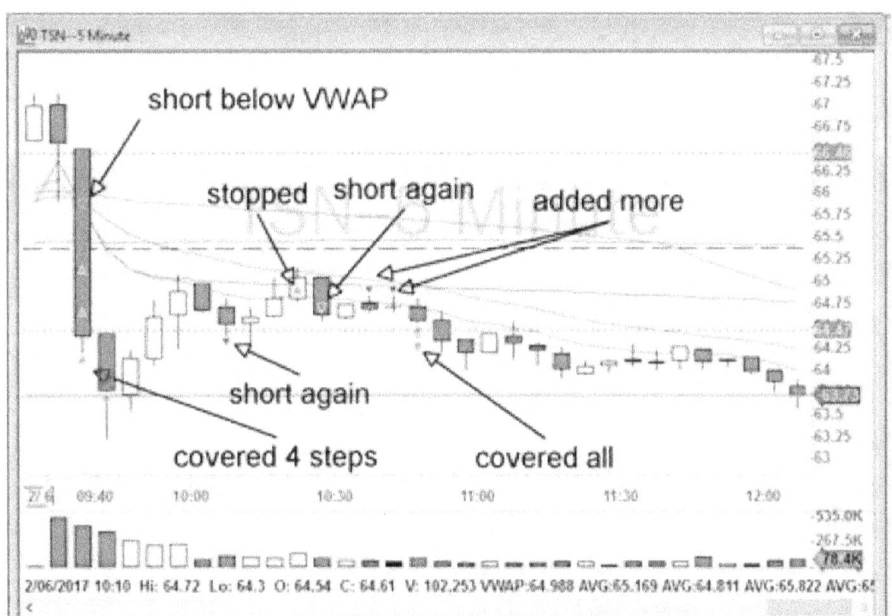

Figure 9.7 - 5-minute chart of TSN on February 6, 2017. I made three trades on it.

Stock is really weak as I am journaling my trades in the morning but I am not going to trade as I hit my daily goal.

HAS

HAS was on my watchlist as well. I went short when stock bounced from high of the day above VWAP, anticipating the break below VWAP. Stock lost the VWAP and I covered my shorts at 9 EMA. Chop Chop!

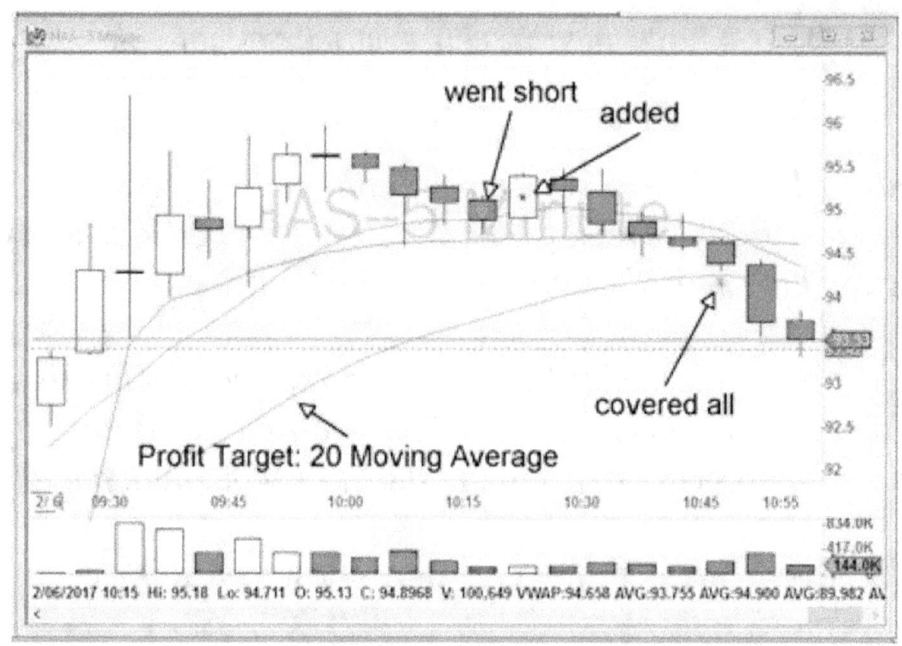

Figure 9.8 - 5-minute chart of HAS on February 6, 2017.

COG

COG was also a short above VWAP. I went short above VWAP and added more as I saw signs of weakness. I covered everything at daily level of $23.45. Chop Chop!

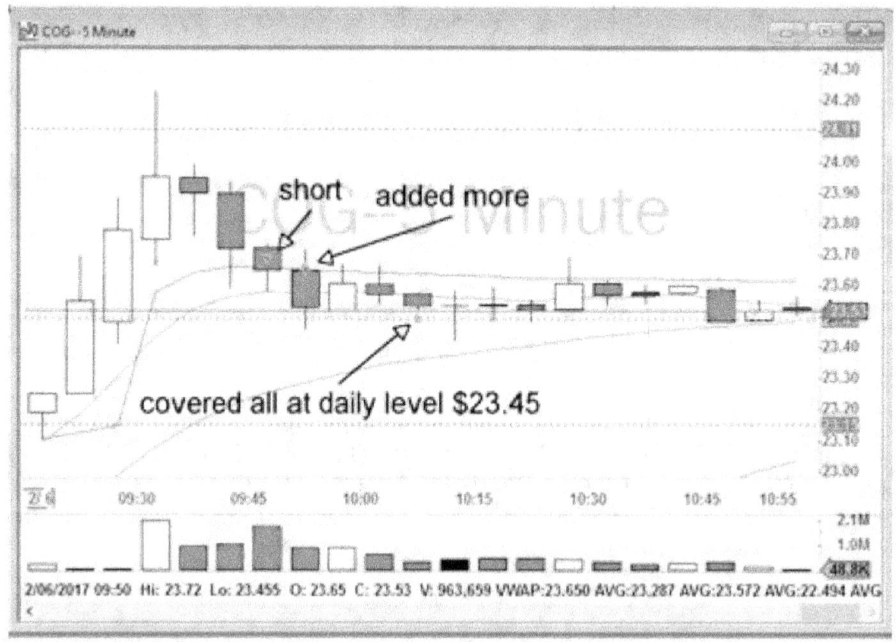

Figure 9.9 - 5-minute chart of COG on February 6, 2017.

It was a good day, +$986!" (as you will see in Figure 9.4 above) ---------

You can read my daily journals on my website. Often traders in my network will discuss my trades with me and I will learn something from them as well. Sometimes I edit videos of my daily trades and post them on my YouTube channel. I keep a library of all of my trading videos and cut and edit them for a trading course that I am currently preparing.

Final Words

You need to practice. You need experience deciphering market patterns and you need to be constantly tweaking your **if-then** statements for your trading setups. Every day is a new game and a new puzzle to solve. Many people believe that trading can be reduced to a few rules that they can follow every morning. Always do this or always do that. In reality, trading isn't about "always" at all; it is about each situation and each trade. You must learn how to think in day trading, and this is no easy task.

You must start recognizing patterns and developing trading strategies. And these strategies must be practiced in real time and under stress. Trading in simulators can help and is absolutely necessary, but there is no substitute for trading with your real hard–earned cash where your results actually matter.

When you begin as a trader, you most likely will be horrible. Many times at the beginning of my career I came to the conclusion that day trading was not for me. Even now that I am an experienced and profitable trader, there is at least one day almost every month that I wonder if I can trade in this market any longer. Of course, this feeling of disappointment goes away faster these days, usually after the next good trade. But for you, because you have not seen success yet, surviving the learning curve is very difficult. I know that. However, this does not mean you should lose a lot of money when you trade live at the beginning. Trading in the simulators will help to prepare you for real trading with real money.

If you are signing up for a training course or mentorship program, you should very carefully read about their plan. A good training program will only encourage you to trade the easiest setups when you start. For example, for the first month live, new traders should only trade Support or Resistance or VWAP trades. The next month, new traders can shift to reversal trades exclusively.

The next month, you should focus on Moving Average Trend trades. After that, you can focus on Bull Flag Momentum plays (momentum trades are the hardest to execute and manage risk in). But you should start with one trade play at a time.

Often new traders expect to make money immediately, and when they don't, they let this affect their work. When they do not see the results that they expected, they start to focus on the wrong things. Some increase their share size, hoping that this will help them make more money. Many will not prepare as hard as they should because they become discouraged. They ask themselves, "What is the point of preparing hard if I cannot make money?" They start to take chances that a successful and experienced trader would never take. They become gamblers. This leads to even more significant losses and only adds to their problem.

While there is no one right way to make money trading, there is only one right way to begin your trading career. When you first begin, you must focus on the process of trading, not on how to make money for a living. You must allow at least eight to twelve months before you will become consistently profitable. If you are not willing or are unable to do this, then you should find another career. Some are not able to either financially or psychologically commit this much time to this pursuit. If this is the case, then again, you should find another profession.

I cannot emphasize enough to you how unimportant the results are from your first six months of trading. They do not matter. During these first months, you are building the foundation for a lifetime career. Do you think in year ten that your results in your first six months will be significant?

I believe becoming a consistently profitable trader just might be the hardest thing you will ever do in your life. Respect the process. You are not entitled to make it. You are entitled to work very hard for eight to twelve months, be trained well, and find out how good you can be. You must believe that you will become great.

Make no mistake, we all have mental weaknesses that we must conquer. Some of us insist in showing the market that we are correct, and we pay the price for that stubbornness. Some cannot accept the loss and exit stocks that trade against them. Some anxiously take small profits when there is no reason to do so and do not wait for the final profit target. Some are afraid to pull the trigger and enter a trade with an excellent risk/reward that they recognize. The only way to get better is to work on your weaknesses.

However, there is no shame in failing as a trader. The real shame is for people who never try to embrace whatever their passion is. If you are passionate about trading, or any other challenge in life for that matter, and you never try it, then you will live your life wondering what could have been. Life is too short to never try new challenges. To try any challenge in life and fail is very honorable.

Having the courage to take a chance and day trade will serve you well later in life. The next career change or next challenge you take may very well be the one to work out for you. What you will learn about yourself in the process is invaluable.

At the end of this book, I have summarized in one place my eleven rules of day trading. I have printed this page off and posted it next to my trading station. I reread it often and I encourage you too as well. I know these rules will help you to keep on track and to be successful.

Last but not least, if you enjoyed reading this book and found it useful, I would very much appreciate your taking a few minutes to write a review on the Amazon website. The success of a book like this is based on honest reviews, and I will consider your comments in making revisions. If you have any feedback, feel free to send me an email. Your review on Amazon will help other people to make informed decisions about my book. I purposely priced it low so more people would be able to purchase it and use it. Teaching people and helping them to start a new career fulfills something inside of me that motivates me every day, so I hope you can help me to accomplish this task of ongoing learning.

If you're ever interested in connecting with me, check out our chatroom at www.BearBullTraders.com or send me an email at andrew@BearBullTraders.com. I'd be happy to have a chat with you.

Thank you, and happy trading!

11 Rules of Day Trading

Rule 1: Day trading is not a strategy to get rich quickly.

Rule 2: Day trading is not easy. It is a serious business, and you should treat it as such.

Rule 3: Day traders do not hold positions overnight. If necessary, you must sell with a loss to make sure you do not hold onto any stock overnight.

Rule 4: Always ask, "Is this stock moving because the overall market is moving, or is it moving because it has a unique fundamental catalyst?"

Rule 5: Success in day trading comes from risk management - finding low-risk entries with a high potential reward. The minimum win:lose ratio for me is 2:1.

Rule 6: Your broker will buy and sell stocks for you at the Exchange. Your only job as a day trader is to manage risk. You cannot be a successful day trader without excellent risk management skills, even if you are the master of many effective strategies.

Rule 7: Retail traders trade only Stocks in Play, high relative volume stocks that have fundamental catalysts and are being traded regardless of the overall market.

Rule 8: Experienced traders are like guerrilla soldiers. They jump out at just the right time, take their profit, and get out.

Rule 9: Hollow candlesticks, where the close is greater than the open, indicate buying pressure. Filled candlesticks, where the close is less than the open, indicate selling pressure.

Rule 10: Indicators only indicate; they should not be allowed to dictate.

Rule 11: Profitable trading does not involve emotion. If you are an emotional trader, you will lose your money.

Glossary

A

Alpha stock: a Stock in Play, a stock that is moving independently of both the overall market and its sector, the market is not able to control it, these are the stocks day traders look for.

Ask: the price sellers are demanding in order to sell their stock, it's always higher than the bid price.

Average daily volume: the average number of shares traded each day in a particular stock, I don't trade stocks with an average daily volume of less than 500,000 shares, as a day trader you need sufficient liquidity to be able to get in and out of the stock without difficulty.

Average relative volume: how much of the stock is trading compared to its normal volume, I don't trade in stocks with an average relative volume of less than 1.5, which means the stock is trading at least 1.5 times its normal daily volume.

Average True Range/ATR: how large of a range in price a particular stock has on average each day, I look for an ATR of at least 50 cents, which means the price of the stock will move at least 50 cents most days.

Averaging down: adding more shares to your losing position in order to lower the average cost of your position, with the hope of selling it at break-even in the next rally in your favor, as a day trader, don't do it, do not average down, ever, a full explanation is provided in this book, to be a successful day trader you must avoid the urge to average down.

B

Bear: a seller or short seller of stock, if you hear the market is bear it means the entire stock market is losing value because the sellers or short sellers are selling their stocks, in other words, the sellers are in control.

Bearish candlestick: a candlestick with a big filled body demonstrating that the open was at a high and the close was at a low, it tells you that the sellers are in control of the price and it is not a good time to buy, Figure 6.1 includes an image of a bearish candlestick.

Bid: the price people are willing to pay to purchase a stock at a particular time, it's always lower than the ask price.

Bid-ask spread: the difference between what people are willing to pay to purchase a particular stock and what other people are demanding in order to sell that stock at any given moment, it can change throughout the trading day.

Black box: the top secret hidden computer programs, formulas and systems that large Wall Street firms use to manipulate the stock market.

Broker: the company who buys and sells stocks for you at the Exchange.

Bull: a buyer of stock, if you hear the market is bull it means the entire stock market is gaining value because the buyers are purchasing stocks, in other words, the buyers are in control.

Bull Flag: a type of candlestick pattern that resembles a flag on a pole, you will see several large candles going up (like a pole) and a series of small candles moving sideways (like a flag), which day traders call consolidating, you will usually miss the first Bull Flag but your scanner will alert you to it and you can then be ready for the second Bull Flag, you can see an example of a Bull Flag formation in Figure 7.3.

Bullish candlestick: a candlestick with a large body toward the upside, it tells you that the buyers are in control of the price and will likely keep pushing the price up, Figure 6.1 includes an image of a bullish candlestick.

Buying long: buying a stock in the hope that its price will go higher.

Buying power: the capital (money) in your account with your broker plus the leverage they provide you, for example, my broker gives me a leverage of 4:1, if I have $25,000 in my account, I can actually trade up to $100,000.

C

Candlestick: a very common way to chart the price of stocks, it allows you to easily see the opening price, the highest price in a given time period, the lowest price in that time period and the closing price value for each time period you wish to display, some people prefer using other methods of charting, I quite like candlesticks because they are an easy-to-decipher picture of the price action, you can easily compare the relationship between the open and close as well as the high and the low price, you can see examples of bearish and bullish candlesticks in Figure 6.1.

Chasing the stock: wise day traders never chase stocks, you chase a stock when you try to purchase shares while the price is increasing significantly, successful day traders aim to enter trades during the quiet times and take their profits during the wild times, when you see a stock surging up, you patiently wait for the consolidation period, patience truly is a virtue!

Chatroom: a community of traders, many can be found on the Internet, as a reader of this book you are welcome to join our www.BearBullTraders.com chatroom.

Choppy price action: stocks trading with very high frequency and small movements of price, day traders avoid stocks with choppy price action, they are being controlled by the institutional traders of Wall Street.

Close: the last hour the stock market is open, 3 to 4 p.m. New York time, the daily closing prices tend to reflect the opinion of Wall Street traders on the value of stocks.

Consolidation period: this happens when the traders who bought stocks at a lower price are selling and taking their profits while at the same time the price of the stock is not sharply decreasing because buyers are still entering into trades and the sellers are not yet in control of the price.

D

Day trading: the serious business of trading stocks that are moving in a relatively predictable manner, all of your trading is done during one trading day, you do not hold any stocks overnight, any stocks you purchase during the day must be sold by the end of the trading day.

Doji: an important candlestick pattern that comes in various shapes or forms but are all characterized by having either no body or a very small body, a Doji indicates indecision and means that a fight is underway between the buyers and the sellers, you can see examples of Doji candlesticks in Figure 6.8.

E

Entry point: when you recognize a pattern developing on your charts, your entry point is where you enter the trade.

Exchange-traded fund/ETF: an investment fund traded on the Exchange and composed of assets such as stocks or bonds.

Exit point: as you plan your trade, you decide your entry point, where you will enter the trade, and you decide where you will exit the trade, if you do not exit properly you will turn a winning trade into a losing trade, whatever you do, don't be stubborn, if a trade goes against you, exit gracefully and accept a loss, don't risk even more money just to prove a point, the markets can be unpredictable.

Exponential Moving Average/EMA: a form of moving average where more weight is given to the most currently available data, it accordingly reflects the latest fluctuations in the price of a stock more than the other moving averages do.

F

Float: the number of shares in a particular company available for trading, for example, in July 2016, Apple Inc. had 5.3 billion shares available.

Forex: the global foreign exchange market where traders – but not day traders – trade currencies.

Fundamental catalyst: this is what you as a day trader are looking for, some positive or negative news associated with a stock such as a FDA approval or disapproval, a restructuring, a merger or an acquisition, something significant that will impact its price during the trading day.

Futures: futures trading is when you trade a contract for an asset or a commodity (such as oil, lumber, wheat, currencies, interest rates) with a price set today but for the product to not be delivered and purchased until a future date, you can earn a profit if you can correctly predict the direction the price of a certain item will be at on a future date, day traders do not trade in futures.

G

Gappers watchlist: before the market opens, you can tell which stocks are gapping up or down in price, you then search for the fundamental catalysts that explain these price swings, and you build a list of stocks that you will monitor that day for specific day trading opportunities, the final version of your watchlist generally has only two, three or four stocks on it that you will be carefully monitoring when the market opens, also called simply your watchlist.

Guerrilla trading: what day traders do, it's like guerrilla warfare, you wait for an opportunity to move in and out of the financial battlefield in a short period of time to generate quick profits while keeping your risk to a minimum.

H

High frequency trading/HFT: the type of trading the computer programmers on Wall Street work away at, creating algorithms and secret formulas to try to manipulate the market, although HFT should be respected, there's no need for day traders to fear it.

High relative volume: what day traders look for in Stocks in Play, stocks that are trading at a volume above their average and above their sector, they are acting independently of their sector and the overall market.

Hotkey: a virtual necessity for day traders, key commands that you program to automatically send instructions to your broker by touching a combination of keys on your keyboard, they eliminate the need for a mouse or any sort of manual entry, high speed trading requires Hotkeys and you should practice using them in real time in a simulator before risking your real money, for your reference I've included as Figure 5.4 a listing of my own Hotkeys.

I

If-then statement/scenario: before the market opens and before you do an actual trade, you should create a series of if-then statements (or if-then scenarios) to guide you in your trade, for example, if the price does not go higher than ABC, then I will do DEF, Figure 9.2 is an example of some if-then statements/scenarios that I have marked on a chart.

Illiquid stock: a stock that does not have sufficient volume traded during the day, these stocks are hard to sell and buy without a significant slippage in price.

Indecision candlestick: a type of candlestick that has similarly sized high wicks and low wicks that are usually larger than the body, they can also be called spinning tops or Dojis and they indicate that the buyers and sellers have equal power and are fighting between themselves, it's important to recognize an indecision candlestick because it may very well indicate a pending price change, you can see examples of indecision candlesticks in Figures 6.6 through 6.8.

Indicator: an indicator is a mathematical calculation based on a stock's price or volume or both, you do not want your charts too cluttered with too many different indicators, keep your charts clean so you can process the information quickly and make decisions very quickly, almost all of the indicators you choose to track will be automatically calculated and plotted by your trading platform, always remember that indicators indicate but do not dictate, Figure 5.2 is a screenshot of the type of chart I use with my indicators marked on it.

Institutional trader: the Wall Street investment banks, mutual and hedge fund companies and such, day traders stay away from the stocks that institutional traders are manipulating and dominating (I'll politely call that 'trading' too!).

Intraday: trading all within the same day, between 9:30 a.m. and 4 p.m. New York time.

Investing: although some people believe investing and trading are similar, investing is in fact very different from trading, investing is taking your money, placing it somewhere, and hoping to grow it in the short term or the long term.

L

Lagging indicator: these are indicators that provide you with information on the activity taking place on a stock <u>after</u> the trade happens.

Leading indicator: a feature of NASDAQ Level 2, it provides you with information on the activity taking place on a stock <u>before</u> the trade happens.

Level 2: successful day trading requires access to the real time NASDAQ TotalView Level 2 data feed, it provides you with the leading indicators, information on the activity taking place on a stock before the trade happens, it provides important insight into a stock's price action, what type of traders are buying or selling the stock and where the stock is likely to head in the near term, Figure 5.1 is an image of a Level 2 quote.

Leverage: the margin your broker provides you on the money in your account, most brokers provide a leverage of between 3:1 to 6:1, a leverage of 4:1, for example, means if you have $25,000 in your account, you have $100,000 of buying power available to trade with.

Limit order: an instruction you give to your broker to buy or sell a specific stock at or better than a set price specified by you, there is a chance the limit order will never be filled if the price moves too quickly after you send your instructions.

Liquidity: successful day traders need liquidity, there must be both a sufficient volume of stock being traded in a particular company and a sufficient number of orders being sent to the Exchanges for filling to ensure you can easily get in and out of a trade, you want plenty of buyers and plenty of sellers all eyeing the same stock.

Long: an abbreviated form of "buying long", you buy stock in the hope that it will increase in price, to be "long 100 shares AAPL" for example is to have bought 100 shares of Apple Inc. in anticipation of their price increasing.

Low float stock: a stock with a low supply of shares which means that a large demand for shares will easily move the stock's price, the stock's price is very volatile and can move fast, most low float stocks are under $10, day traders love low float stocks, they can also be called micro-cap stocks or small cap stocks.

M

Margin: the leverage your broker gives you to trade with, for example, if your leverage is 4:1, if you have $25,000 in your account, your margin to trade with is

$100,000, margin is like a double-edged sword, it allows you to buy more but it also exposes you to more risk.

Margin call: a serious warning from your broker that you must avoid getting, your broker will issue you a margin call if you are using leverage and losing money, it means your loss is equal to the original amount of money in your account, you must either add more money to your account or your broker will freeze it.

Marketable limit order: an instruction you give to your broker to immediately buy or sell a specific stock within a range of prices that you specify, I use marketable limit orders when day trading, I generally buy at "ask+5 cents" and I sell at "bid-5 cents".

Market cap/market capitalization: a company's market cap is the total dollar value of its float (all of their shares available for trading on the stock market), for example, if a company's shares are worth $10 each and there are 3 million shares available for trading (a 3 million share float), that company's market cap is $30 million.

Market maker: a broker-dealer that offers shares for sale or purchase on the Exchange, the firm holds a certain number of shares of a particular stock in order to facilitate the trading of that stock at the Exchange.

Market order: an instruction you give to your broker to immediately buy or sell a specific stock at whatever the current price is at that very moment, I'll emphasize the phrase "whatever the current price is", the price might be to your benefit, it very well might not be though.

Medium float stock: a stock with a medium float of between 5 million and 500 million shares, I mostly look for medium float stocks in the range of $10 to $100 to trade, many of the strategies explained in this book work well with medium float stocks.

Mega cap stock: a stock with a huge supply of shares, for example, Apple Inc. had 5.3 billion shares available for trading in July 2016, their stock prices are generally not volatile because they require significant volume and money to be traded, day traders avoid these types of stocks.

Micro-cap stock: a stock with a low supply of shares which means that a large demand for shares will easily move the stock's price, the stock's price is very volatile and can move fast, most micro-cap stocks are under $10, day traders love micro-cap stocks, they can also be called low float stocks or small cap stocks.

Mid-day: 11 a.m. to 3 p.m. New York time, the market is generally slow at this time with less volume and liquidity, it's the most dangerous time of the day to be trading.

Moving average/MA: a widely used indicator in trading that smooths the price of a stock by averaging its past prices, the two basic and most commonly used MAs are the Simple Moving Average (SMA), which is the simple average of a stock over a defined number of time periods, for example 1-minute, 5-minute, or daily charts, and the Exponential Moving Average (EMA), which gives more weight to more recent prices, the most common applications of MAs are to identify the trend direction and to determine support and resistance levels, I use 9 EMA, 20 EMA, 50 SMA and 200 SMA on all of my charts, your charting software will have most of the types of MAs already built into it.

O

Open: the first 1.5 hours the stock market is open, 9:30 to 11 a.m. New York time.

Opening range: when the market opens, Stocks in Play will often experience what I call violent price action, heavy trading will impact the price of the stock, I quite like a 5-minute opening range to determine what direction the price is heading towards and whether the buyers or sellers are winning, others will be equally successful waiting for a 15-minute or 30-minute opening range.

Options: a different type of trading, it's trading in contracts that gives a person a right, but not a duty or requirement, to buy or sell a stock at a certain price by a specific date.

Over-the-counter (OTC) market: most day traders do not trade in the OTC market, it's a specific market used to trade in such items as currencies, bonds and interest rates.

P

Pattern Day Trade Rule: a regulation in the United States that requires day traders in the United States to have at least $25,000 in their account unless they use a non-U.S. based broker, it does not impact day traders who live in Canada, England, or any other country other than the United States.

Penny stock: the shares of small companies that can trade at very low prices, the prices can be very easily manipulated and follow no pattern or rule whatsoever, fraud is rampant in penny stock trading, day traders do not trade penny stocks.

Position sizing: refers to how large of a position you can take per trade, it's a technique and skill that new traders must develop but, please remember one of my rules, you must never risk more than 2% of your account in any one trade.

Pre-market trading: trading that takes place before the market officially opens at 9:30 a.m. New York time, I personally avoid pre-market trading because since so few traders are trading, you have to trade in very small share sizes, if you are considering pre-market trading, you should check with your broker to see if they permit it, with all of that said though, it's useful to keep an eye on pre-market trading, a stock that is gapping up or down by 2% or more in the pre-market definitely gets my attention and may make my watchlist for the day.

Previous day close: the price of a stock when the market closes on the previous day, knowing the previous day close of a stock is a useful tool for gauging if a stock may come into play the following day and it is a figure used in a number of strategies and patterns explained in this book.

Price action: the movement in price of a stock, I prefer using candlesticks to chart the price action of a stock, capturing its highs and lows and the relationship between the open and close.

Profit target: as a day trader, you should have a daily profit target and once you reach it, don't be greedy and risk it, you can turn off your computer and enjoy the rest of your day, in addition, for each trade you set up, you should have a specific profit target that your strategy is based upon.

Profit-to-loss ratio: the key to successful day trading is finding stocks that have excellent profit-to-loss ratios, these are the stocks with a low-risk entry and a high reward potential, for example, a 3:1 ratio means you will risk $100 but have the potential to earn $300, a 2:1 ratio is the minimum I will ever trade, also called risk/reward ratio or win:lose ratio.

R

Real time market data: to be a successful day trader, you need access to real time market data (that you usually must pay for), without any delay, as you will be making decisions and entering and exiting trades literally in minutes, swing traders on the other hand, who enter and exit trades within days or weeks, need only have access to end-of-day data, and that data is available for free on the Internet.

Relative Strength Index/RSI: a technical indicator that compares the magnitude of recent gains and losses in the price of stocks over a period of time to measure the speed and change of price movement, your scanner software or platform will automatically calculate the RSI for you, RSI values range from 0 to 100, an extreme RSI below 10 or above 90 will definitely catch my interest.

Retail trader: individual traders like you and I, we do not work for a firm and we do not manage other people's money.

Risk management: one of the most important skills that a successful day trader must master, you must find low-risk trading setups with a high reward potential, each trading day you are managing your risk.

Risk/reward ratio: the key to successful day trading is finding trading setups that have excellent risk/reward ratios, these are the trading opportunities with a low-risk entry and a high reward potential, for example, a 3:1 ratio means you will risk $100 but have the potential to earn $300, a 2:1 ratio is the minimum I will ever trade, also called profit-to-loss ratio or win:lose ratio.

S

Scanner: the software you program with various criteria to find specific stocks to day trade in, Figures 4.2 to 4.5 are screenshots of the scanners I often use.

Short: an abbreviated form of "short selling", you borrow shares from your broker, sell them, and hope that the price goes even lower so you can buy them back at a lower price, return the shares to your broker and keep the profit for yourself, to say "I am short AAPL" for example means you have sold shares in Apple Inc. and are hoping their price goes even lower.

Short interest: the quantity of shares in a stock that have been sold short but not yet covered, it is usually reported at the end of the day, I generally do not trade stocks with a short interest higher than 30%, a high short interest means that traders and investors believe a stock's price will fall.

Short selling: you borrow shares from your broker and sell them, and then hope the price goes even lower so you can buy them back at the lower price, return the shares to your broker and keep the profit for yourself.

Short Selling Restriction/SSR: a restriction placed on a stock when it is down 10% or more from the previous day's closing price, regulators and the Exchanges place restrictions on the short selling of a stock when its price is dropping, when a stock is in SSR mode, you are still allowed to sell short the stock, but you can only short when the price is going higher, not lower, intraday.

Short squeeze: occurs when the short sellers panic and are scrambling to return their borrowed shares to their brokers, their actions cause prices to increase quickly and dangerously, you want to avoid being stuck short in a short squeeze, what you do want to do is ride the squeeze when the price quickly reverses.

Simple Moving Average/SMA: a form of moving average that is calculated by adding up the closing price of a stock for a number of time periods and then dividing that figure by the actual number of time periods.

Simulator: it's mandatory for new day traders who wish a successful career to trade in a simulator for several months, you should purchase a simulated account that provides you with real time market data and you should only trade in the share volume and with the amounts of money you will actually be trading with when you go live, simulators are an excellent way to practice using your Hotkeys, to practice creating if-then statements and to practice (and practice some more) your strategies.

Size: the "size" column on your Level 2 will indicate how many standard lots of shares (100 shares = 1 standard lot) are being offered for sale or purchase, a "4" for example means 400 shares.

Small cap stock: a stock with a low supply of shares which means that a large demand for shares will easily move the stock's price, the stock's price is very volatile and can move fast, most small cap stocks are under $10, some day traders love small cap stocks but do note that they can be really risky, they can also be called low float stocks or micro-cap stocks.

Spinning top: a type of candlestick that has similarly sized high wicks and low wicks that are usually larger than the body, they can be called indecision candlesticks and they indicate that the buyers and sellers have equal power and are fighting between themselves, it's important to recognize a spinning top because it may very well indicate a pending price change, Figures 6.6 and 6.7 are examples of spinning tops.

Standard lot: 100 shares, the "size" column on your Level 2 will indicate how many standard lots of shares are being offered for sale or purchase, a "4" for example means 400 shares.

Stock in Play: this is what you as a day trader are looking for, a Stock in Play is a stock that offers excellent risk/reward opportunities, it will move higher or lower in price during the course of the trading day and it will move in a way that is predictable, stocks with fundamental catalysts (some positive or negative news associated with them such as a FDA approval or disapproval, a restructuring, a merger or an acquisition) are often Stocks in Play.

Stop loss: the price level when you must accept a loss and get out of the trade, the maximum amount you should ever risk on a trade is 2% of your account, for example, if your account has $10,000 in it, then you should never risk more than $200 on a single trade, once you calculate the maximum amount of money you can risk on a trade, you can then calculate your maximum risk per share, in dollars, from your entry point, this is your stop loss, your stop loss should always be at a reasonable technical level, in addition, you must honor your stop loss, do not change it in the middle of a trade because you hope something will happen, gracefully exit your trade and accept the loss, do not be stubborn and risk your account.

Support or resistance level: this is the level that the price of a specific stock usually does not go higher than (resistance level) or lower than (support level), stocks often bounce and change the direction of their price when they reach a support or resistance level, as a day trader you want to monitor these levels because if your timing is correct you can profit from that rapid change in price direction, I provide some detailed commentary in this book on how to find support and resistance levels, the previous day close is one of the most powerful levels of support or resistance, Figure 7.23 is an example of a chart that I have drawn support and resistance lines on.

Swing trading: the serious business of trading stocks that you hold for a period of time, generally from one day to a few weeks, swing trading is a completely different business than day trading is.

T

Ticker: short abbreviations of usually one to five letters that represent the stock at the Exchange, all stocks have ticker symbols, Apple Inc.'s ticker for example is AAPL.

Trade management: what you do with your position when you enter a trade and before you exit it, you don't just sit patiently in front of your computer screen with your fingers crossed for good luck and watch what happens, as you monitor and process the information that is changing in front of you, you must adjust and fine tune the trade you are in, you must be actively engaged in your trade, the only practical way to gain experience in trade management is in a simulator, using the share volume and actual amounts of money you will one day be trading with live.

Trade plan/trading plan: the plan you develop before you actually enter a trade, it takes hard work to develop a solid trade plan and to then practice sufficient self-discipline to stick with the plan, see also the definition for if-then statement/scenario.

Trading platform: a software that traders use for sending orders to the Exchange, brokers will offer you a trading platform that is sometimes for free but often for a fee, platforms are either web-based or as a software that needs to be installed on your computer, your trading platform provides your charting and order execution platform, having a good trading platform is extremely important as it needs to be fast and able to support Hotkeys and excellent charting capabilities, I myself use and recommend DAS Trader, I pay a monthly fee to access their platform and real time data.

V

Volume Weighted Average Price/VWAP: the most important technical indicator for day traders, your trading platform should have VWAP built right into it, VWAP is a moving average that takes into account the volume of the shares being traded at any given price, while other moving averages are calculated based only on the price of the stock on the chart, VWAP considers the number of shares in the stock being traded at each price, VWAP lets you know if the buyers or the sellers are in control of the price action.

W

Watchlist: before the market opens, you can tell which stocks are gapping up or down in price, you then search for the fundamental catalysts that explain these price swings, and you build a list of stocks that you will monitor that day for specific day trading opportunities, the final version of your watchlist generally has only two, three or four stocks on it that you will be carefully monitoring when the market opens, also called your Gappers watchlist.

Win:lose ratio: the key to successful day trading is finding stocks that have excellent win:lose ratios, these are the stocks with a low-risk entry and a high reward potential, for example, a 3:1 ratio means you will risk $100 but have the potential to earn $300, a 2:1 ratio is the minimum I will ever trade, also called profit-to-loss ratio or risk/reward ratio.